Advance Praise for
Teaching with Conscience in an Imperfect World

"In *Teaching with Conscience in an Imperfect World*, Bill Ayers makes a compelling and passionate plea for ending prejudice, bias, and systematic deception toward youth in our schools. How can our children reasonably believe in adults at school when they are regularly deprived of their own immediate experiences, interpretations, intellectual curiosity, and joy? However routinized by our test-driven culture, a profound level of soul-loss is at stake—and with equally acute implications for our children's well-being. This captivating text takes the reader on an emancipatory journey toward a brighter educational future replete with hope and multiple, redemptive possibilities."

—Angela Valenzuela, author of *Subtractive Schooling;*
professor, College of Education, University of Texas at Austin

"*Teaching with Conscience in an Imperfect World* offers energized democratic thinking: 'freedom dreams' and 21 other great ideas that resist the current climate of neoliberalism where only numbers count. Bill Ayers invites you to imagine teaching in ways that make a difference; ways that bring smiles and successful learning to students and joyous fulfillment to teachers."

—Carl Grant, Hoefs-Bascom Professor of Education,
School of Education, University of Wisconsin, Madison

"A timely read that lifted my spirits for the work to be done. Thanks. . . . I needed this book."

—Deborah Meier, teacher, principal, writer, and advocate, recipient of
MacArthur "Genius" Award for her work in New York City's East Harlem

"I could not put this book down, eager to accompany a journey sparked by questions that both unravel and recenter. William Ayers' *Teaching with Conscience in an Imperfect World* takes readers on a journey through autobiography, history, literature, sociology, philosophy, to delve deeply behind the common sense of today, to imagine what schooling could look like, be for, and aim towards. Accept the invitation to imagine, embrace the contradiction that is education for democracy, and find yourself building what we were never schooled to build."

—Kevin Kumashiro, author of
Bad Teacher! How Blaming Teachers Distorts the Bigger Picture;
dean and professor, School of Education, University of San Francisco

"In this exhilarating, invigorating, and uplifting book, William Ayers invents an exciting pedagogical creed for our times. He calls on all educational workers to teach courageously and creatively, to liberate human potential, to exercise our radical imaginations, and to cultivate hope in this increasingly complicated and contested world."

—Ming Fang He, professor, Georgia Southern University

"The great Civil Rights leader Fannie Lou Hamer talked about being sick and tired of being sick and tired. This book is for every classroom teacher who is challenged by what they fear is a dark time for public schools in America. This book is for every classroom teacher who is sick and tired of being sick and tired of prescriptive solutions to problems we don't recognize and answers to questions we never asked. Bill Ayers reminds us again that teaching can be an act of art, subversion, and imagining what is possible."

—Fred Klonsky, retired public school teacher,
education blogger at FredKlonsky.com

"Through critical and hopeful prose, Bill Ayers reveals the questions educators of conscience ask themselves in their quiet time. In a tumultuous time where much is uncertain, I remain thankful for his challenge to continue to transform those quiet moments into something bold and loud enough to move us towards justice."

—David Stovall, professor, University of Illinois at Chicago

"Advice to new teachers falls into one of two camps: Reproduce the status quo or wage a lonely struggle against it. Bill Ayers presents us with a third path. Paved with imagination, lined with playfulness and leading toward freedom, Ayers invites those of us committed to educational justice to join him with fresh eyes, open hearts, and creative spirits. This book will provide preservice students and practicing teachers with unique ways to digest the depth of what they're up against, while inspiring them to joyfully design and collectively construct what is yet to be."

—Bree Picower, associate professor, Montclair State University

"To be quite honest, what I recommend is that on those days when we teachers feel like we just can't be in those rooms anymore doing what they tell us to do, we need to pick up Teaching with Conscience, tuck it under our arms, and carry it around with us all day like a damn Linus blanket. Every so often we should then refer to it and be reminded how to love teaching again, how to love ourselves as teachers again, and how to never stop loving the kids.

This magnificent ode to the true intent and purpose of education should be required reading for every parent, young person in high school, and teacher entering a teacher education program. Instead of certification exams, let's challenge teachers to design what Ayers inspires us to create: a realistic 'vision of learning communities that no one will have to suffer through' and 'schools that kids won't need to recover from.' Teaching with Conscience offers us a true test of our will to love young people. Can we pass it?"

—Lisa Arrastia, founder and director, The Ed Factory

TEACHING WITH CONSCIENCE
IN AN IMPERFECT WORLD

◇◇◇◇◇◇◇◇◇◇◇

an invitation

William Ayers

TEACHERS COLLEGE PRESS

TEACHERS COLLEGE | COLUMBIA UNIVERSITY

NEW YORK AND LONDON

Published by Teachers College Press, 1234 Amsterdam Avenue, New York, NY 10027

Cover and interior art by Nathaly Bonilla

Library of Congress Cataloging-in-Publication Data

Names: Ayers, William, 1944– author.
Title: Teaching with conscience in an imperfect world : an invitation / William Ayers.
Description: New York, NY : Teachers College Press, [2016] | Includes bibliographical references.
Identifiers: LCCN 2015048162
ISBN 9780807757918 (pbk. : alk. paper)
ISBN 9780807757925 (hardcover : alk. paper)
Subjects: LCSH: Critical pedagogy–United States. | Social justice–Study and teaching–United States. | Teachers–Professional relationships–United States.
Classification: LCC LC196.5.U6 A95 2016 | DDC 370.11/5–dc23
LC record available at http://lccn.loc.gov/2015048162

ISBN 978-0-8077-5768-0 (paper)
ISBN 978-0-8077-7479-3 (ebook)

Printed on acid-free paper
Manufactured in the United States of America

23 22 21 20 19 18 17 16   8 7 6 5 4 3 2 1

To the brave explorers of the far horizons:
Dalin Alexi, Light Ayli, and Jacai Michael

Contents

Series Foreword

Teaching for social justice might be thought of as a kind of popular education—of, by, and for the people—something that lies at the heart of education in a democracy, education toward a more vital, more muscular democratic society. It can propel us toward action, away from complacency, reminding us of the powerful commitment, persistence, bravery, and triumphs of our justice-seeking forebears— women and men who sought to build a world that worked for us all. Abolitionists, suffragettes, labor organizers, civil rights activists: Without them, liberty would today be slighter, poorer, weaker— the American flag wrapped around an empty shell—a democracy of form and symbol over substance.

Rousseau argues in regard to justice that equality "must not be understood to mean that degrees of power and wealth should be exactly the same," but only that with respect to *power*, equality renders it "incapable of all violence" and only exerted in the interest of a freely developed and participatory law, and that with respect to *wealth*, "no citizen should be so opulent that he can buy another, and none so poor that he is constrained to sell himself." The quest for equality and social justice, over many centuries, is worked out in the open spaces of that proclamation, in the concrete struggles of human beings constructing and contesting all kinds of potential meanings within that ideal. Nothing is settled, surely, once and for all, but a different order of question presents itself. Who should be included? What do we owe one another? What is fair and unfair?

This series gathers together examples of popular education being practiced today, as well as clear and new thinking concerning issues of democracy, social justice, and educational activism. Many contributions will be grounded in practice, and will, we hope, focus on the complexities built into popular education: difficulties, set-backs, successes, steps forward—work that reminds us of what Bernice Johnson Reagon calls "the sweetness of struggle." We also seek developing theoretical work that might push us all forward as we look for new meanings of democracy in changing times, the demands of justice, and the imperatives of social change. We want to encourage new voices and new ideas, and in all cases to contribute to a serious, grounded, and thoughtful exchange about the enduring questions in education: Education for what? Education for whom? Education toward what kind of social order?

For every human being life is, in part, an experience of suffering and loss and pain. But our living experience also embraces other inescapable facts: that we are all in this together, and that much (but not all) of what we suffer in life is the evil we visit upon one another—that is, unjustified suffering, unnatural loss, unnecessary pain—the kinds of things that ought to be avoidable, that we might even imagine eliminating altogether.

In the realm of human agency and choice, we come face to face with some stubborn questions: Can we stop the suffering? Can we alleviate at least some pain? Can we repair any of the loss? We lurch, then, toward deeper considerations: Can society be changed at all? Is it remotely possible—not inevitable, certainly, perhaps not even very likely—for people to come together freely, to imagine a more just and peaceful social order, to join hands and organize, to struggle for something better, and to prevail?

If society cannot be changed under any circumstances, if there is nothing to be done, not even small and humble gestures toward something better, well, that about ends all conversation. Our sense of agency shrinks, our choices diminish. What more is there to say? But if a fairer, saner, and more just social order is both desirable and possible—that is, if some of us can join one another to imagine and build a participatory movement for justice, a public space for the enactment of democratic dreams—our field opens slightly. There would still be much to be done, for nothing would be entirely settled. We would still need, for example, to find ways to stir ourselves and our neighbors from passivity, cynicism, and despair; to reach beyond the superficial barriers that wall us off from one another; to resist the flattening effects of consumerism and the blinding, mystifying power of the familiar social evils—racism, sexism, and homophobia, for example; to shake off the anesthetizing impact of most class-rooms and most research, and of the authoritative, official voices that dominate the airwaves, the media, and so much of what we think of as common sense; to, as Maxine Greene says, "release our imaginations" and act on behalf of what the known demands, link-ing our conduct firmly to our consciousness. We would be moving, then, without guarantees, but with purpose and with hope.

Education is, of course, an arena of struggle as well as hope—struggle, because it stirs in us the need to reconsider everything we have wrought, to look at the world anew, to question what we have created, to wonder what is worthwhile for human beings to know and experience, to justify or criticize or bombard or maintain or build up or overthrow everything before us—and hope, because we gesture toward the future, toward the impending, toward the com-ing of the new. Education is where we gather to question whether and how we might engage and enlarge and change our lives, and it is, then, where we confront our dreams and fight out our notions of the good life; where we try to comprehend, apprehend, or possibly even change the world. Education is contested space, a natural site of conflict—sometimes restrained, other times in full eruption—over questions of justice.

The work, of course, is never done. Democracy is dynamic, a community always in the making. Teaching for social justice con-tinues the difficult task of constructing and reinvigorating a public. It broadens the table, so that more may sit together. Clearly, we have a long, long way to go. And we begin.

—William Ayers, Series Editor;
Therese Quinn, Associate Series Editor

ONE

◇◇◇◇◇◇◇◇◇◇◇◇◇◇◇◇◇◇◇◇◇◇◇◇◇◇◇◇

Imagine a world that could be, or a world that should be, but isn't apparent or available to us just yet. Dream a little—what would a better world look like? Now imagine coming together with others and trying to create or build that possible or conceivable world. It's work to be sure—sometimes really, really hard work—this imagination business, but it's also an enduring heritage, a distinctly human quality that "ignites the slow fuse of possibility," as Emily Dickinson wrote.

Engaging the imagination involves mapping the world as it really is, and then purposely stepping outside the known and the established in order to lean toward a world that *could be*, but is not yet. This is the dynamic work of lighting that fuse: rejecting the fixed and the stable and the predictable, and reaching toward an alternative, stretching toward the possible. This is where we search for something better, and where we nourish our freedom dreams. This is when the imagination blows up.

The magnificent Chicago poet Gwendolyn Brooks begins her "Dedication to Picasso," an homage to the great man and the huge sculpture that he gave to our city, asking whether "man" does indeed love art. Her answer is that we visit art but flinch and draw back. The reason is, she explains, that art hurts—it "urges voyages."

The voyages demanded by art lie at the very heart of our humanness: journeys in search of new solutions to old problems, explorations of spirit spaces and emotional landscapes, trips into the hidden meanings and elaborate schemes we construct to make our lives understandable and endurable, flights hooked on metaphor and analogy, wobbly rambles away from the cold reality we now inhabit toward an indistinct but beckoning world beyond. These are the voyages that foreground the capacities and features that mark us as uniquely *human* beings: invention, aspiration, self-consciousness, projection, desire, ingenuity, moral reflection and ethical action, courage and compassion and commitment. All of these and more are the vital harvests of our imaginations.

But it's also true that those speculative rambles can hurt. The capacity to see the world as if it could be otherwise unleashes yearning and liberates desire—we are freed (or condemned) to run riot. Our lively imaginations can be rowdy, tending toward disruption and subversion; opening up alternatives always calls the status quo into question. Suddenly the taken-for-granted becomes a choice and not an echo, an option and no longer a habit or a life (death) sentence. The seeds of discontent are sown.

How do we see our schools right here, right now? How do we make sense generally of the educational system today? Are we conscientiously and systematically teaching free people to participate fully in a free society? In what ways? Could we do a better job of encouraging young people to interrogate the world fully, to ask deeper questions and to pursue those questions to their furthest limits? Do we intentionally and openly help children and youth develop minds of their own? And do we simultaneously offer students opportunities to be responsible and participating members of their communities? What can we imagine our schools being or becoming that they are not yet? How might we get there?

Perhaps even more important, how can we live purposefully in the schools as they are while we stretch toward something new and dramatically better—schools that are more joyful and more just, more hopeful and more loving? And how can we build within ourselves the capacity and the courage, the thoughtfulness and compassion to dive into the wreckage on a mission of repair?

In 1897, after months of illness and suicidal despair, the tormented French painter Paul Gauguin produced a sprawling panorama on a huge piece of coarse jute sacking, an image of unfathomable figures amid scenery that might be the twisted groves of a tropical island or a marvelously wild Garden of Eden. There are worshipers and gods, cats, birds, and a quiet goat, a great idol with a peaceful expression and uplifted hands, a central figure plucking fruit, and a depiction of what must be Eve—not as a voluptuous innocent like most of Gauguin's women, but as a shrunken hag with an intense eye.

Gauguin scrawled the title of his creation in bold over the image; translated into English it reads: "Where do we come from? What are we? Where are we going?" These questions were troubling and terrifying for Gauguin, struggling with his sanity in the whirlwind of modernity. For us, though, these questions may prove indispensable—our provocative and propulsive little accomplices. They provide the frame for what follows.

◇　◇　◇

Imagine if you and I were elected to be part of a large planning commission charged with envisioning and designing a contemporary school system for children and their families in a wildly diverse, newly formed community—not a single school but an entire system of schools, from kindergarten through high school. We are asked to bring an open mind to the task in the spirit of the original call: We're willing to learn and to share, we'd pledged, before we were elected, to investigate and study, to speak with the possibility of being heard and to listen with the possibility of being changed. Our approach would be dialogue not monologue, a quest not a conquest, and so we would seek consensus wherever possible and compromise whenever necessary.

Each of us would bring our unique histories, experiences, and distinct perspectives to the process, of course, but we would also encourage ourselves to bracket our preconceptions, to dream large and to create something from the bottom up, beyond habit and familiarity, beyond the easy assumption that the way things are is simply "*the way it's spozed to be,*" something entirely natural and somehow inevitable. Where should we start? Think big. What would you propose first? And then what? It's a wide-open space, you know, a huge and empty canvas, so think even bigger.

I've asked students from urban public high schools to small rural boarding schools to take a moment, breathe in and breathe out, relax, and go a little starry-eyed with me: "If you had the power to upend and reform anything in your school," I would say, "anything at all, what would you change?" This, it turns out, is a tougher question to wrap our minds around than you might think at first. A few irreverent students get easy laughs from their comrades with a quick response: "I'd fire Ms. Truslow," or "I'd ditch the National Anthem and have kids hookup a new mixtape onto the PA every morning to get things started right."

More typical responses include things like better food in the lunch room, longer passing periods between classes, or more holidays and a school schedule that begins at, say, 10 A.M. These reform suggestions, sound and satisfactory on their face, strike me as fatally stuck in the mud. I'd said, "Storm the Heavens!" "Change anything!" and the responses tended toward better baloney in the cafeteria. How puny. How bloodless.

I'm not blaming the students at all—the frame of their experiences sets the initial horizon of their thinking, and that's true for all of us. In this case the basic anatomy of "school" is a fixed idea in most of our minds, a structure and skeleton entirely predictable and fundamentally immutable, a shadow that hovers and then envelops most of the available space. Asked to alter anything at all, our imaginations stall and then shut down, and our ideas amount to a rearranging-the-deck-chairs-on-the-Titanic type of reform. We have a tough time escaping the prison of received wisdom and conventional thinking. There may be better ways to ask the question or more robust prompts to prod all of us toward rethinking and reforming schools—and much of that is the focus of what follows—but to begin, it's worth noting that school is, well, *school* after all—it will always be, we assume, as it's always been. We're inclined to shrug our shoulders, palms up in surrender.

I recently served on an architectural jury charged with selecting the winning proposals in a national school-design competition. Architects, who are part artists, part engineers, and part philosophers rolled into one, typically exercise their imaginations more than most of us as part of their everyday professional activities, and there were several breathtakingly beautiful designs in the hundred-plus submissions, a few that were daring and innovative:

a nature trail through an urban high school, an outdoor theater space on an oddly shaped rooftop. In discussion with the other jurors, mostly architects, I learned a lot about "universal design," environmental standards, and green and sustainable structures. But I also witnessed once again the crippling weight of conformity whenever the talk turned to *school* itself.

There were continual references in the design write-ups asserting that the space under consideration had been conceived and fashioned to engage the "whole person" and to teach "critical thinking," and each design team claimed that their creation offered a uniquely "student-centered" environment. But for all the familiar rhetoric, there was a depressingly backward-looking sameness when it came to considering alternatives to the way typical schools have been hatched and managed for more than a century. In the hands of these otherwise creative and boundary-breaking architects, "student-centered," to take one hot example, simply meant developing a curriculum that could be downloaded onto laptops and completed at a pace and in a place of the student's choosing. There was no real palpable sense of tapping into the experiences, glory, or stubborn agency of youth, and so we were offered student-centeredness in strictly mechanical and technocratic terms.

The so-called choice was so anemic and narrow—go fast or go slow, sit in the classroom or stand on your head in the hallway, but the curriculum is already planned by wise and benevolent people, and you must run the course as it is—that from the perspective of the student it was pure illusion amounting to no choice at all; it was a distinction without a difference. In this "student-centered" universe there was no consulting on content, no accounting for the plans and desires of youth, no sense of the wisdom or energy they might be willing to unleash and share in the classroom or the community. These schools looked a lot like occupying colonial powers delivering civilization itself into the assumed empty territory of students' minds.

Returning to the community planning commission, imagine if I kicked off the conversation at our first meeting by proposing that school funding be vastly uneven, and that one school should be offered a new state-of-the-art campus, generous resources, and fantastic materials, while another school just down the street would be housed in an abandoned warehouse with broken windows and a busted furnace, and receive but a pittance. The commission members might begin looking at one another uneasily, shaking their heads in mild disbelief. "Wait! There's more!" I'd cry, hurriedly elaborating my plan: In the first school, class size would be limited to 15, while in the other it would be allowed to balloon up to 40 or more students per teacher. What? And, I'd go on to explain, the schools would be strictly segregated by class and race and family income—the wealthy school overwhelmingly White, the under-resourced school mostly Black or Latino/a. Commission members are moving steadily away from me now, and I can't figure out why—these are, after all, the schools I've known my whole life, the system as it actually is in my hometown. I continue a little desperately: "Come back! You haven't heard the best parts yet, the bits about how students of the privileged get a curriculum of question-asking and problem-posing, while the others are monitored obsessively and disciplined with a high-tech electronic management app, and how compliance is guaranteed—any deviation from the rules or procedures and the misfits will be immediately forced out of school. And about how we will measure inputs and outputs and cognitive growth at the end of each day. Why are you all leaving?"

Bertrand Russell once said that every person "is encompassed by a cloud of comforting convictions, which move with him [or her] like flies on a summer day." The comforting convictions about schools include the bells and the public address system, of course, the classes and the schedules and the elaborate management schemes, but most important, the conviction that there is—and *must be*—a rigid hierarchy of teachers and learners in place. This evokes Paulo Freire's vivid metaphor of the "banking model" of education, and we picture a child's mind as a fat but empty piggy bank: The teacher deposits knowledge into the little slot on top, and the students are filled up over time; the teacher acts and the students are acted upon; the teacher knows everything and the students know little or nothing; the teacher teaches and the students are taught; the teacher thinks and the students are thought about; the teacher talks and the students listen; the teacher disciplines and the students are disciplined; the teacher is a subject with a will and a mind and a sense of agency, while the students are mere objects. These beliefs and premises constitute an inflexible and insistent common sense: They *are* that cloud of summer flies. And this is exactly the problem: The cloud of flies asks no questions, seeks no evidence, demands no reasons or arguments, and invites no dialogue. They simply buzz around incessantly.

Swatting the flies away and dreaming big is clearly no simple assignment—we are entangled and weighed down by the heavy chains of uniformity and conformity, silenced by the rigid authoritative voice of convention. Because we live day by day immersed in what *is*—the world as such—imagining a landscape much different from what's immediately before us requires a combination of somethings: seeds, surely; desire, yes; effort, of course, always effort; idealism and romance, maybe; necessity and desperation at times; and a vision of possibility at other times. Occasionally what's required is the willful enthusiasm to dance out on a limb.

That's what this little book is about. It's a provocation to stretch and to reach, and an invitation to enthusiastically dance out on that limb. It's an incitement to participate in collectively unleashing our unruly imaginations, outlining a vision of what schools should be and perhaps could be. And it's a come-on: hold hands, close your eyes, go wild, and get utopian.

TWO

◇◇◇◇◇◇◇◇◇◇◇◇◇◇◇◇◇◇◇◇◇◇◇◇◇◇◇◇◇◇◇◇◇

Where do we come from? When searching for someone lost in the wild, trackers start from a spot they identify as the "Point Last Seen." Since the wilderness is vast and the wanderer or camper or skier could be almost anywhere, the searchers gather at the last known sighting and fan out from there—the Point Last Seen is where we come from.

Before we ramble too far into the backcountry—planning to get a little lost ourselves, but entirely on purpose, and in a good way—it makes sense to note our own Point Last Seen and sketch the school territory we're angling away from since we'll be leaving for the wilds soon enough.

Let's start back in the 19th century, at the dawn of what we think of as the modern institution of school, at Charles Dickens's memorable introduction in *Hard Times* to the aptly named Mr. Gradgrind, the owner of a school in an industrial city, and Mr. M'Choakumchild, his hired schoolmaster. Here Gradgrind lectures M'Choakumchild on his philosophical orientation and a few of the finer points of curriculum and instruction:

> Now, what I want is, Facts. Teach these boys and girls nothing but Facts. Facts alone are wanted in life. Plant nothing else, and root out everything else. You can only form the minds of reasoning animals upon Facts: nothing else will ever be of any service to them. This is the principle on which I bring up my own children, and this is the principle on which I bring up these children. Stick to Facts, Sir!
>
> The speaker, and the schoolmaster . . . swept with their eyes the inclined plane of little vessels then and there arranged in order, ready to have imperial gallons of facts poured into them until they were full to the brim.

To deepen and illustrate his argument, Gradgrind interrogates "girl number twenty," and, discovering that her father is a horseman, asks her to define a horse. When she stumbles, Gradgrind pounces: "Girl number twenty unable to define a horse. . . . Girl number twenty possessed of no facts, in reference to one of the commonest of animals!" He turns to a boy who obediently stands and recites: "Quadruped. Graminivorous. Forty teeth, namely twenty-four grinders, four eye-teeth, and twelve incisive . . ." And on and on, at the end of which Gradgrind nods approvingly and notes, "Now girl number twenty, you know what a horse is."

Girl number twenty—Sissy Jupe, by name—indeed knows quite a lot about horses, of course, and a number of other things as well. She's a three-dimensional person with agency and a mind and a spirit, a heart and a body, experiences and hopes and dreams just like every other human being. She has compassion for others and a fine sense of aesthetics, and she has a broad imagination, which she calls her "Fancy," all qualities Gradgrind finds irrelevant or repellent. Facts, Sir!

In these opening chapters of *Hard Times*—one appropriately called "The Murder of Innocents"—Dickens evokes the broad outlines of autocratic classrooms everywhere. He offers a kind of meditation on the power of these men of facts-without-feeling to crush or twist our natural human dispositions and sympathies, and he turns at last to M'Choakumchild himself with an indictment: "When . . . thou shalt fill each jar brim full by-and-by, dost thou think that thou wilt always kill outright the robber Fancy lurking within—or sometimes only maim him and distort him!"

Dickens's fraught description of a tyrannical classroom in England under the rule of Queen Victoria is oddly familiar, and for that very reason quite surprising—we might imagine that education and schooling in a contemporary democracy would look remarkably different from a British classroom 160 years ago. Monarchies, after all, demand unquestioning allegiance first and foremost, whereas democracies, at least theoretically, are built on the active engagement and participation of free and enlightened people. And because schools no matter where or when are always mirror and window into whatever social order creates and sustains them, we can easily imagine the society that the above-mentioned "imperial gallons of facts" are meant to sustain and reproduce; what's harder to reconcile is an inescapable feeling that Dickens' despotic classroom with its imperious reasoning and its brute logic is a bit too close for comfort.

◇   ◇   ◇

So let's pay critical attention to our own classrooms, and look unblinkingly for a moment at educational policy and schools today: For example, in 2006 Florida passed the Florida Education Omnibus Bill, stipulating that "American history shall be viewed as factual, not as constructed, shall be viewed as knowable, teachable, and testable." The bill called for an emphasis on the "teaching of facts." Facts and only facts—without "fancy" or frivolous and messy interpretations—would be permitted by the legislators to enter the schoolhouse. Facts and only facts would be allowed to guide instruction about, for example, the "period of discovery." I read that and did a neck-wrenching double-take: Huh? Whose facts, exactly, I wondered? The facts of a Genoan adventurer in the pay of Spanish royalty; the facts of the "discovered" themselves with their complex stories of tribal rivalries, resistance, and accommodation; the facts of the First Nations residents overwhelmed, murdered, and enslaved; or possibly a range of other facts and angles-of-regard altogether? I'll guess that the Gradgrinds among the Florida lawmakers went with the first choice, legislating in effect a pep-rally for Christopher Columbus—yes, their own particular *constructed* explanation and analysis of events and circumstances passing as Fact. Still it's deeply bizarre and mindlessly pinheaded to banish debate and dialogue, independent inquiry and first-hand research, and the right to think for oneself in a hurried scramble to paint a prettified picture of freedom and democracy in the name of Fact. Never mind: Teach the Facts! Stick to Facts, Sir!

In 2008 a group in the Arizona legislature passed a law stating that schools whose curriculum and teaching "denigrate or encourage dissent" from "American values" risked losing their state funding. But, you might say, dissent is the first and foremost American value, etched into our consciousness from day one, and American history is nothing if not a long, unfolding story of defiance and refusal, protest and resistance from the revolutionaries of 1776 onward: Abolitionists, Suffragettes, anarchists and labor pioneers, civil rights and Black Power warriors, peace and environmental activists, feminists, heroes and sheroes and queeroes, Wounded Knee, Occupy, Black Lives Matter! Wherever you look and whatever period you examine, questioning authority and taking it to the streets is as American as cherry pie, an apple-core American value, and the very engine of forward progress—except to the Gradgrinds of Arizona. Never mind! FACTS! And nothing but the facts!

In 2015 Wisconsin Governor Scott Walker proposed to change the century-old mission of the University of Wisconsin system— known from the start as the Wisconsin Idea—by removing words that instructed the university to "search for truth" and "improve the human condition"—vague, fanciful, and open to any number of constructions, conflicts, contradictions, and interpretations—and replace them with "meet the state's workforce needs." That's more down-to-earth, more practical.

Also in 2015 David Coleman, head of the College Board and a leading standards-bearer, said in a talk about the Common Core State Standards that teaching personal writing in high schools— the exposition of an opinion or the development of a personal narrative—was not particularly important. Students engaging in the age-old work of searching and questioning, wondering and wandering on the page was beside the point, he said, and largely irrelevant to the task of being forged into a fact-filled, test-ready, workforce-oriented fragment and scrap of humanity. His exact words—"people really don't give a shit about what you feel or what you think"—were catapulted via YouTube into an instant viral phenomenon, easily found online.

At about the same time and in an identical spirit the College Board revised its guidelines for teaching Advanced Placement History, which have broad influence in high school history courses

(Klein, 2015): "Manifest Destiny" has become more benign in the retelling, the phrase "American Exceptionalism" is used for the first time, and violence against Native Americans is downplayed. The Republican National Committee had urged Congress to stop funding the College Board, saying it "emphasizes negative aspects of our nation's history while omitting or minimizing positive aspects." Whew! Now that that's fixed, the modern-day Gradgrinds, who seem to be loose everywhere on the land, can move along to sniffing out other deviant and subversive thoughts that may be lurking beneath every rock.

In almost every area and from almost every quarter, we discover a giddy, lemming-like rush toward a curriculum of facts: incontrovertible "Truths," uncontested and measurable, inarguable and beyond dialogue or debate. Legislatures and school boards stipulate what students must know and be able to do, and what teachers must teach. Students are regularly and increasingly measured by a set of predetermined standards—with high-stakes standardized tests, of course—on precisely what they know and are able to do, and teachers must be held accountable for what students know and are able to do. In Illinois, for example, the legislature has decreed that 30% of a Chicago teacher's evaluation is to be based on students' standardized test scores.

The whole scheme can be made to sound rational and straightforward, and in certain board rooms and policy conferences it can easily win the day. But as we shall see later, it also undermines the core of what it means to be an educated person in a free and democratic society. For now, though, note: critical thought—banished; interpretation or analysis—gone; that "robber Fancy"—humbug; Gradgrind and M'Choakumchild—triumphant!

Facts: I watched a history teacher in a Southside Chicago school offer a standard lesson on the legendary 1954 Supreme Court case *Brown v. Board of Education* that reversed *Plessy v. Ferguson* and ended racial segregation in the United States. The classroom was made up of 24 African-American students and seven Latino/a students. The lesson was pointedly directed toward illustrating our great upward path as a nation. A student who had appeared to me to be paying no attention at all spoke up rather suddenly, smiling broadly as he addressed the teacher: "So you're saying this class here is against the law? We're breaking the law here, right? Can I call the cops?" Everyone cracked up, but the disruptive student was pointing to an obvious contradiction: Here was a segregated class-room in a segregated school in a country that had outlawed school segregation decades ago.

A brilliant high school teacher in the city of Baltimore by the name of Jay Gillen outlines a range of responses that might occur to that teacher teaching *Brown v. Board of Education* in a racially segregated space, because he has found himself in similar situations again and again: patriotic ("Segregated schools no longer exist in America. This country is great."); ironic ("I have to mouth this offi-cial doctrine, but we all understand this doctrine is a lie."); devoted ("We must continue . . . making the promise of Brown more real in the coming decades."); moralizing ("You students of color should appreciate the advances that have been made by taking advantage of the opportunities offered to you to receive an education."); ob-jective ("The . . . ruling was read May 17, 1954. . . . Remember that much for the test."); Black nationalist ("We're better off in this seg-regated space."). Gillen's list is far from exhaustive, but his laying bare the contradiction is on point.

It doesn't take perceptive young people any time at all to sniff out the duplicity and the dirty-dealing in the nothing-but-the-facts agenda and to conclude that all schools lie. Teachers lie. Parents lie. In fact, the whole edifice of adult society is a complete phony, a tangled and fiddly fraud sailing smoothly along on a sea of silence. Many students submit to the empire of deception, concluding that it's simply the price of the ticket: You wink at the massive hoax and promise to keep quiet and go along, and you'll pick up your reward by and by. Many other students go in the opposite direc-tion: Their insights lead them to insurgent actions and gestures and styles, all matter-of-fact performances of self-affirmation and hard-nosed refusals of complicity—flat-out rejections of a world that is determinedly disinterested in their aspirations and perceptions and insights.

There's a genre of jokes that all end with the same punch line: In one version, a man comes unannounced and unexpectedly upon his partner in the intimate embrace of another, and explodes in accusation. The accused looks up indignantly and says, "Who are you going to believe—me? or your own lying eyes?" Kids get it viscerally: schools are asking them to ignore their immediate experiences and their direct interpretations—to discount their own lying eyes. Who are you going to believe?

In her dazzling experimental novel *The Golden Notebook,* Nobel Laureate Doris Lessing (2008) offers a compelling statement about modern education as a dominion of deception:

> It may be that there is no other way of educating people. Possibly, but I don't believe it. In the meantime it would be a help at least to describe things properly, to call things by their right names. Ideally, what should be said to every child, repeatedly, throughout his or her school life is something like this:

> "You are in the process of being indoctrinated. . . . We are sorry, but it is the best we can do. What you are being taught here is an amalgam of current prejudice and the choices of this particular culture. The slightest look at history will show how impermanent these must be. You are being taught by people who have been able to accommodate themselves to a regime of thought laid down by their predecessors. It is a self-perpetuating system . . . you [must] find ways of educating yourself—educating your own judgment . . ." (p. xxii)

Too many schools and classrooms run along on the rails of indoctrination and propaganda: the hype that the curriculum is settled and complete, and the spin about children and youth who are regularly "thingified"—turned into objects—mistrusted and controlled, subjected to an alphabet soup of negative labels (LD, BD, EMH, ODD) that are putatively accurate and telling, and defined as lacking in many of the essential qualities that make one fully human. This cries out for reimagination and resistance, rethinking and rebuilding.

◇   ◇   ◇

On a daily basis and as part of the normal routine too many schools endorse the failure of too many students—especially children of the least powerful politically—in the name of responsibility and objectivity and consequences. For these and many other students the experience of schooling is easily summed up: Nothing of real importance is ever a part of classroom life, nothing is connected to anything else, nothing is completely forthright and honest, nothing is pursued to its furthest limits, nothing is ever undertaken with investment or courage, and not much of lasting value is ever accomplished. In an odd way, too many schools seem to celebrate ignorance, insisting that matters of real importance to students be banned (too controversial, too youthful, too diversionary) and that the present period be worshiped as a point of arrival rather than as a dynamic and fleeting moment, like any other. Most schools fetishize rules, control, standardization, conformity, facts, and order, rather than honoring, say, freedom, inquiry, divergence, variation, creativity, beauty, novelty, flexibility, improvisation, and uniqueness. Most obsess about what Natalia Ginzburg has called "the little virtues"— things like thrift, caution, and a longing for material success—at the expense of the great virtues: generosity, courage, love, a desire to know and to *be*.

Few classrooms invite students to ask any serious questions: What's the evidence? How do we know? Whose viewpoint is being privileged and whose is being ignored or left out? Who is visible and who is missing or silenced? Who benefits and who suffers? What are the alternatives, the connections, the resistances, the patterns, the causes? Where are things headed? Why? Who cares? It's no surprise, then, to find schools enveloped in a culture of complaint and cynicism, suffocating in a pervasive air of purposelessness, irrelevance, and fatalism. While the marginalized are punished, even the successful students are mildly miserable—they are too often taught the collateral lessons of how to fake it, how to cheat, how to cut corners, and how to get by without any passion for, or commitment to, anything. Those attitudes bend toward cynicism and narcissism, and can easily become habits to drag into future jobs and personal relationships, into the rest of their lives.

In a free society education must be both public and democratic; this is essential to the creation of democracy's public spaces and humanity's culture of community. The right to a free and public education, for example, is enshrined in every state constitution in the United States, a prestigious standing not granted other aspects we might include in our sense of life, liberty, and the pursuit of happiness—such as housing, employment, or health care.

And here is a basic contradiction: We know how to teach children well—the social science and the research is in, folks—but in the United States (as in most places in the world) we do so unequally. We have terrific schools with dazzling facilities and state-of-the-art materials, a curriculum that encourages engaged thinking and active curiosity, and great outcomes for students that are both anticipated and admirable. But these schools are clustered in well-off communities where folks have the cultural currency and the economic and political capital to have them built; money is disproportionately showered on the already-privileged. So we know what's possible, and we also know where it's likely (and where unlikely) to be brought to life in practice. A visitor from Mars observing all this might conclude that we have a rather cynical policy regarding children, and it can be summed up quite simply: Choose the right parents! If you choose the right parents you'll have access to good food and excellent health care, adequate housing and well-resourced schools, police who act like public safety officials rather than an occupying army, clean air and sound neighborhoods and decent recreational opportunities. If you pick the wrong parents, well . . . sorry. Bad idea. You're on your own.

◇   ◇   ◇

In our public conversation and our political debates education is increasingly, and a bit too glibly, cast as a product like a laptop or a printer—something bought and sold in a marketplace like any other commodity. It's a powerful image: schools as businesses run by CEOs, teachers as the workers on the assembly line, and students as the raw materials bumping along the conveyor belt as information is incrementally stuffed into their empty up-turned heads—neat and rational and efficient. The market metaphor can be overpowering, stretching out in every direction: "Downsizing" the least productive units while "outsourcing" and privatizing a space that once belonged to the public becomes a natural event; teaching toward a simple standardized metric and relentlessly applying state-administered (but privately developed and quite profitable) tests to determine the "outcomes" becomes a rational proxy for learning; the organized and collective voice of teachers becomes cast as irrelevant at best and more likely a self-serving and destructive chorus of whiners; centrally controlled "standards" for curriculum and teaching are made to seem commonsensical; "zero tolerance" for student misbehavior as a stand-in for child development or justice becomes normal; crude competition becomes a commanding motivator for learning; and "accountability," that is, a range of sanctions on students, teachers, and schools—but never on law-makers, foundations, or corporations—becomes logical and level-headed.

Federal policy—No Child Left Behind, Race to the Top—has been built on an uncritical embrace of this metaphor. Education, which is naturally cooperative and communal, has been encouraged by Congress and the White House, law and policy, to become a vicious swamp fight among the reptiles for the meager available resources: It's my state against your state, it's my school against your school, and it's my 3rd grade against your 3rd grade. The curriculum narrows to only those things that will be tested; after all, if my job depends on my 3rd-graders outscoring your 3rd-graders, what possible motivation do I have to share teaching insights, strategies, or resources? This approach incentivizes swindling and fraudulent claims at every level: It's me alone against all of you—and the whole wide world. And this explains why cheating scandals on student standardized tests are rampant (and entirely predictable) across the land from Atlanta to Lake Forest to Washington to San Diego, and why the Department of Education is barking up the wrong tree when it hires a former FBI director to get to the bottom of things and secure the tests at all cost. The problem isn't security; it's the wrong incentives and questionable goals.

Education as directed by national politicians today is a weapon in a new "Cold War," a struggle of all against all. This is not new; when I was a junior high school student, the nation had gone nuts over the Soviet Union launching Sputnik—"school reform" meant getting more serious about science and math in order to catch up with and then crush the Russians.

I began teaching 8 years later, in 1965, and school reform was again on the agenda—this time, reflecting the social landscape, tilting toward racial integration, multicultural curriculum, and the full inclusion of girls and women in all school matters.

A couple of decades later, as I was doing research for my doctorate, school reform under Ronald Reagan's Department of Education was front and center, cast now as an alarming national security issue: "If an unfriendly foreign power had attempted to impose on America the mediocre educational performance that exists today, we might well have viewed it as an act of war." A Nation at Risk declared that "the educational foundations of our society are presently being eroded by a rising tide of mediocrity that threatens our very future as a Nation and a people."

That was 1983, but the urgency never lets up: We are always and everywhere reforming our schools; it's as regular as rain in Seattle.

That's not to say that I think that school reform is either frivolous or pointless. I share a sense of urgency with other reformers, and I have a deeply held faith that people working together can indeed transform our public schools—even the whole of society—into spaces of purpose and productivity for all young people. But I note that school reform has a long and uneven history.

And now we are being led into a bizarre moral panic: Help! Rise up! Don't allow China (India, Brazil, South Africa, Japan, Russia) to out-educate us or to get ahead of us in the knowledge wars!

The inducement and inspiration to succeed in school is increasingly fashioned as a battle, and frankly I strain to imagine any 3rd-grader struggling through her homework in the evening with this mantra playing over and over in her head: Must outscore 8-year-olds in Shanghai! Must outscore little girls in Calcutta!

In this market-driven, hypercompetitive scenario the Secretary of Education becomes not an educational leader for the nation's children and youth, but an adjunct to the Secretary of Commerce and a cheerleader for international business. Or, still in a cheerleading outfit, the Secretary is like a junior program officer at a gleaming foundation dispensing grants only to the most worthy, those who write what she or he judges to be the loveliest top-tier proposals. There will be, of course, some lucky winners perched triumphantly upon the bent backs of the many losers. The implications of this domineering—but always contested—metaphor are staggering.

The sorry list of Secretaries of Education stretches back decades— T. H. Bell and William Bennett, Margaret Spellings and Rod Paige, Richard Riley and Lamar Alexander, Arne Duncan and John King— and while educators might find it easier to have a designated bogeyman, in reality misdirected, inappropriate school policy has been an entirely bipartisan affair. An inventory of federal strategies and practices is troubling at best: a mad frenzy of testing in classrooms across the country as if high-stakes, standardized test scores are the goal rather than a single (and inadequate) measure of educational outcomes; a ballooning practice of evaluating teachers based on student test scores, causing massive demoralization, plummeting enrollments in teacher education programs including Teach for America, and skyrocketing early retirement rates among veterans; billions of dollars spent on promoting a dual school system of privately managed charter schools operating alongside neighborhood or community public schools; the steady rise of an aggressive privatization effort bent on eliminating public education altogether in urban districts where residents have the least political power; the systematic resistance of many new charter schools to enroll the neediest children; escalating rates of racial resegregation; expanding voucher programs that transfer public funds to religious schools; the spread of exploitative for-profit colleges preying on veterans and minorities, and plunging students into crippling debt.

This is not the whole story, of course, and it's nothing personal—a critical catalog like this points to policy, not personality.

◇   ◇   ◇

Testing has been a common cudgel in the hands of the powerful, a kind of modern and scientized eugenics device. But it has unleashed a forceful opposition from parents and communities as well: Opt Out! The Opt-Out Movement—parents electing to have their children skip the tests, stay home, or sit in the auditorium during test time—speaks to a deep discomfort with and mistrust of the dominant testing regimen. One of the worst things about the testing system—and parents and teachers witness this at close order—is that it labels some kids "losers" and others "winners" while they are very young. That's a tragedy for all of them, and over time it will become a catastrophe for the larger society—and for the possibility of an agreeable social order. Many families and entire communities have concluded that not only are the tests expensive and disruptive but they have no authentic educational benefit; and many folks are becoming more sophisticated in analyzing the relative value of high-stakes standardized testing. One of the clearest objections is that the weight placed on certain measures, combined with the huge consequences (i.e., high stakes) makes gaming the system—that is, fudging and cheating—inevitable.

This insight is variously called "Goodhart's Law" after the British economist Charles Goodhart, or the "Heisenberg Principle of incentive design" after the uncertainty principle at the heart of quantum physics: "a performance metric is only useful as a performance metric as long as it isn't used as a performance metric" (Porter, 2015). I love that, and, put simply, it means that announcing a policy up front with significant rewards and punishments tied to a specific measure—a measure meant to stand for an entire universe of interest—will always result in people working exclusively on that designated measure, usually to the detriment of the larger goals. Presbyterian Hospital lowered mortality rates (the universe) by working feverishly to keep patients alive for 31 days after surgery, thereby beating by a day Medicare's survival measurement (the performance metric). Similarly, Urban Prep built a reputation as a good school (the universe) because it sent 100% of its graduates to college (the performance metric) while covering up a massive push-out rate and a suspect list of what counts as "college." This also explains why cheating scandals on student standardized tests are rampant across the land from Atlanta to Lake Forest to San Diego, and why the Department of Education is barking up the wrong tree when it hires a former FBI director to get to the bottom of things and secure the tests at all cost. The problem isn't security, it's assuming a performance metric is useful as a performance metric.

It's also the age-old problem of starting in the wrong place—the testing machine can test only specific things, and those specific testable things then become glorified as the things-most-needful. The tail once again is wagging the dog. Albert Einstein famously noted that not everything that can be counted counts, and not everything that counts can be counted. Think: love, joy, justice, beauty, kindness, compassion, commitment, effort, interest, engagement, awareness, connectedness, happiness, sense of humor, relevance, honesty, self-confidence, respect for others, and . . . keep counting.

In a clever cartoon by Randy Glasbergen that became a popular Internet meme, a teenager matter-of-factly tells his astonished mother, "I got an 'A' in my business class. I outsourced my homework to a kid overseas."

High-stakes standardized tests typically fail to link back to teachers in any meaningful way, which means that they're useless as tools of formative evaluation—that is, they don't help teachers teach better, and because that's so, they kind of miss the point. Furthermore, test results typically correlate with income and educational levels of families, which means that they are first and foremost a measure of zip codes and a test of class backgrounds and therefore a kind of massive fraud that asks everyone to act as if you "earned" your scores in an objective, context-free world. The students most harmed by high-stakes standardized tests tend to be the least standard among us.

◇   ◇   ◇

Multiple Choice Question:

A typical American classroom has as much to offer an inquiring mind as does:

    a. a vacant lot
    b. a back alley
    c. a street corner
    d. the city dump
    e. an oil spill
    f. **none of the above**

Analogy Question:

High-stakes, standardized testing is to learning as:

    a. memorizing a flight manual is to flying
    b. watching an episode of *CSI: Miami* is to doing police work
    c. exchanging marriage vows is to a successful relationship
    d. reading *Grey's Anatomy* is to practicing heart surgery
    e. singing the national anthem is to citizenship
    f. **all of the above**

The correct answer to each of these hypotheticals is "f". In the multiple choice question the answer is "none of the above" because each of the options listed offers, not "as much" material and provocation to an inquiring mind, but significantly more; in the analogy test the answer is "all of the above" because all of the activities described—memorizing, watching, singing—fail to correlate to the desired outcomes, just as testing fails to meaningfully correspond to learning.

◇   ◇   ◇

A quick way to opt out of both the Common Core State Standards and the high-stakes standardized testing frenzy is to send your kids to a boarding school like Exeter or Andover or to a prep school like Washington's Sidwell Friends or the University of Chicago Laboratory Schools (Lab), founded over 100 years ago by John Dewey. Lab is the expensive private school Arne Duncan went to and the school his own kids attend. Other notable parents include Barack and Michelle Obama, Richard Daley (former mayor), Rahm Emmanuel (current mayor), and (what the heck) me! This is a school where teachers—with a strong and forceful union—are not evaluated a whit by student test scores, the hammer of tests is nonexistent, class size is limited to 18 students, libraries and media centers abound, sports and games are available for a range of abilities and interests, resources are rich, and a full program of the many arts is flourishing. And here is a staggering hypocrisy: as the whip hand of educational policy, the President, the Secretary of Education, and the Mayor ask for nothing close to any of that when it comes to *your* kids.

This insincerity is typical and endemic among the current crop of corporate reformers: None of their kids go to the drill-and-kill schools they're designing and building for other people's children. To me—and feel free to argue with me here—this reflects a deeply upper-class bias and assumption that the children of the elite are more fully human and more altogether deserving than other children, especially children of Black or Brown poor people. Inequality is an epidemic in U.S. schools, but the market metaphor allows the powerful to dodge or ignore that core fact, going forward day by day, piously framing the school discussion in corporate terms, ignoring and belittling entire communities, demonizing teachers, treating students as objects of endless manipulation.

John Dewey opposed this phenomenon a century ago. Whatever the wisest and most privileged parents in a democracy want for their children, he argued, must serve as a minimum standard for what we as a community want for all of our children. Any other ideal for our schools, he said, "is narrow and unlovely; acted upon, it destroys our democracy."

What if this school/classroom/experience were for me, or for my precious children? This can be an illuminating starting point for discussion: If it's not OK to cut the arts or sports programs, the clubs or libraries or science labs for your child—or for the children of privilege—how can that be OK for someone else's children? If the elite want teachers for their kids who are thoughtful, caring, compassionate professionals—well-rested and well-paid, completely capable of making clear and smart judgments in complex and unpredictable situations—how can they in good conscience advocate for teachers who are little more than mindless clerks for the children on the other side of town? We should be highly skeptical of reformers who claim to know what's best for other people's children—whether Gates or Bloomberg or Bush or Obama—when it would be completely unacceptable for them or for their treasured wee ones. In a democracy everyone is the one of one, each induplicable and entirely precious. Contrast the schools built for the highly privileged with the schools for the 99%—the results may be predictable, but this is a fair and reasonable test, easy to run in any state or city or town, more telling and relevant than student standardized test scores, and important to publicize. Our response to any attempts to rationalize or explain away these glaring inequities can be two little words borrowed from the corporate reformers, and redeployed in the service of justice: No excuses!

All metaphors are imperfect, of course, yet their task is always the same: to advance interesting and important insights by providing a lateral perspective and a unique or unexpected point of view. But this metaphor—education as capitalist corporation—adds nothing of value to our understanding of the enterprise. Instead it commandeers the discussion about schools and school improvement, yanking our attention away from the real issues we need to face, forcing us far afield on every important dimension—it misunderstands how human beings learn; it misreads teaching and how teaching actually works; it finesses the central place of inequality and poverty and structural racism in student outcomes with pseudoscientific, fictitious objectivity and a culture of competition that assumes and expects many losers; and it dismisses the crucial role communities must play in the education of the young, all of which I'll get to later. But the metaphor is indeed what a range of notably powerful people, noisy politicians, and chattering, cheerleading pundits have embraced and christened "school reform," and they defend it forcefully, hammer and claw.

◇ ◇ ◇

The obsessions that characterize American classrooms today—especially urban classrooms and schools attended by the poor, recent immigrants from impoverished countries, First Nations peoples, and the descendants of formerly enslaved people—are simple: The goal is obedience, standardization, and conformity; the watchword, "Control." These schools are characterized by passivity and fatalism and infused with anti-intellectualism, dishonesty, and irrelevance. They turn on the familiar technologies of constraint—ID cards, uniform dress codes and regulations, surveillance cameras, armed guards, metal detectors, random searches—and the elaborate schemes for managing the fearsome, potentially unruly, mob. The knotted system of rules, the exhaustive machinery of schedules and clocks and surveillance, the unaesthetic physical space and prison architecture, the laborious programs of regulating, indoctrinating, inspecting, disciplining, censuring, correcting, counting, appraising, assessing and judging, testing and grading—all of it makes this feel like an institution of punishment, not of enlightenment and liberation, a place to recover from rather than an experience to carry forward.

A *New Yorker* cover from September 11, 2000 gets it partly right: A severe-looking man in a long coat is walking down a street holding leashes attached to collars around the necks of eight subdued children; the piece is called "Obedience School." The only off-note is that the little ones are all white and preppy-looking.

The M'Choakumchilds and Gradgrinds of today dress up in suits and speak a mystifying half-language of social science research—they look, in fact, a lot like a movie version of a smug and satisfied Secretary of Education or an eager, well-scrubbed charitable foundation officer entirely confident in his own good intentions—but their task is pretty much the same: separating the successful from the failures, sorting and managing the masses, and ensuring that all children more or less submissively accept their proper place in the hierarchy of winners and losers and, with that, their lot in life.

Here we might ask specifically and concretely how centrally generated standards and an extensive testing regime, for example, or eliminating the arts, or replacing career teachers with a steady parade of short-timers specifically in urban and low-income areas—all "reforms" that the schools of the privileged manage to avoid—do anything to improve education for each and for all. The satirical *Onion* captured this last piece—inner-city teaching as a heartening if brief tourist destination for recent college graduates—flawlessly in one of its "Point/Counterpoint" features: In the first photo a perfectly privileged-looking young woman smiles happily into the camera and the headline announces, "My year of working with underprivileged kids, and how it made me a better person"; the Counterpoint is represented by an exasperated-looking 4th-grader of color asking, "When am I going to get a real teacher in this school?"

And one of the best parodies of this entire reform metaphor is a short piece from MAD–TV available on YouTube called *Nice White Lady*. It opens as a camera hovers over an urban landscape and the narrator intones: "The American urban high school. . . . There's nowhere more dangerous. . . . Out of control students, parents who don't give a damn, lazy incompetent teachers. . . ." The camera enters a classroom where kids of color are lounging at their desks cleaning their firearms and sharpening their knives. The narrator again: "What can possibly save them?" The door creaks open a crack and a young, fresh-faced woman peeks in and announces, "Hi, I'm Amy Little; I'm a nice white lady and I'm here to help you." The kids sneer and jeer, and one young woman is right up in her face with maximum urban attitude: "What the fuck you know 'bout me, bitch?" she growls, as she rattles off a series of horrid events in her life. Amy is at first taken aback, but then a light bulb goes off, and she hands the student a pen and notebook with the command: "Write that down!" Soon everyone is writing and winning literary awards, trading their guns for pencils. As they all dance together in the hallway, the narrator concludes: "So if you want to improve the schools, you don't need more resources or better curriculum. . . . All you need is a nice white lady."

When education and schools are cast as items for individual consumption, and nothing more—neither a public trust nor a social good, and certainly not a fundamental human right—learning becomes something like boots or hammers; unlike boots and hammers, the value of which is inherently satisfying and directly understood, the value of school learning is elusive and indirect. Its value, we're assured, has been calculated elsewhere by beneficent rulers, putatively wise and accomplished people with our best interests at heart, and these Gradgrinds and M'Choakumchilds must surely know better than anyone what's best for *these* kids (remember: it's always for other people's children and never their own) and for the world at large. "Take this medicine," students are told repeatedly, day after tedious day, "It's good for you." Refuse that bitter pill and go stand in the corner—where all the other losers are assembled. Management, inputs and outcomes, efficiency, cost controls, profit and loss, measurable outcomes—this is the domineering language that leaves little room for doubt and not much space to think differently.

None of this can be very good for us. It may be our Point Last Seen, but it's not an inevitable landscape nor an inescapable prison. We will soon begin to plot our escape, picturing schools as palaces of learning and classrooms as spaces where the desires and yearnings of youth can be deployed with energy and focus. We will break from the boot-camp metaphor that guarantees failure for far too many youngsters as we make our wobbly way out of the wreckage and toward the schools of our dreams. The wilderness beckons, urging us to start moving and searching.

What follows will track that quest as we sketch more fully and fill in more completely a vision of what could be, what we might reach for, where the sparkling bits of possibility can be found now. As we join hands and head for the hills we'll need to breathe in the good air and breathe out the bad, to keep on breathing, growing, stretching, blooming and flourishing, emerging, thriving, unfolding, developing. All of it is our birthright—this whole wild business of being alive and on the move.

THREE

◇◇◇◇◇◇◇◇◇◇◇◇◇◇◇◇◇◇◇◇◇◇◇◇◇◇◇◇

What are we? After months of planning and waiting, and after hours of concentrated labor—relentless effort and sweat and pain—our first child was born in our bed in our fifth-floor walk-up apartment. It was, of course, like every birth, a small miracle—the heroic, triumphant new mother; that tiny giant baby shimmering through blood and goo, sputtering and then announcing himself full force; the magical midwife cleaning and swaddling him in a twinkling, passing Zayd over to Bernardine who, though exhausted, looked dazzling and delirious, tripping on the immense journey she'd just shared with her blessed child and gazing at him through a veil of tears. She stroked his face and spoke his name for the first time before putting him to her breast.

Each of us is the embodiment of that miracle and that gift, and this is the first and fundamental answer to the question of what we are: we are each of woman born. We are each worthy of empathy, each mortal.

You can surely imagine the scene: Bernardine had prepared steadily for the birth and for this moment—she had practiced and rehearsed, exercised and stretched, listened to the advice of peers and elders, read books and eaten healthy new-mom food, manically cleaned and prepared the nest, and even joined La Leche League. She is at this moment teaching Zayd how to nurse. But look more closely and you might notice something subtle and all but imperceptible from the outside: While Bernardine is holding his head and guiding his mouth, Zayd is readjusting, pushing back, and telling her things she didn't get from books or friends. The teacher is becoming the student of the student, and the student is, amazingly, a teacher of the teacher.

Zayd is all of 5 minutes old, and yet he's assuming the teacher role with his mom; he knows things about his life that she cannot possibly know. Think of the teacher he could become—the expert on his own life and feelings and needs and desires, the explorer and discoverer—at 5 years old, or at 15, or 25. That is, if we expect it and allow it.

Mother and child are negotiating this moment together, the first intense consultation in what will become a series of urgent conversations in the weeks and months ahead. And yes, Bernardine is teaching him all the while to nurse; and, yes, Zayd is teaching her, too—and therein lies the glory: the first intimate dialogue has begun, and in this dialogue, each participant is both an attentive student as well as an engaged, committed teacher. This is profoundly human and powerful learning—innate and immediate, self-directed and shared, natural, authentic, spirited, passionate, direct and discursive, multidimensional, vital and ongoing.

Learning is living in its most basic sense. The baby and the mother are motivated by the desire to live—simple, yes, but far-reaching and complex as well. We are learning beings because we are living human beings. To be human is to learn; to learn is to live. This, too, is what we are.

And we're learning all the time, but note (and I'll say more about this later), we're not always learning those things that will make us stronger, more confident and more powerful in our projects or our pursuits, more capable of becoming central actors in society or, if we choose, more able to dramatically transform it. Just as we can learn to trust, we can learn to mistrust; we can learn shame and doubt as well as confidence, passivity as well as industry. These kinds of negative learnings are possible and all too common, and they are not useful for a life of growth and fulfillment—they shut down the life force of learning that leads inevitably and relentlessly toward deeper and further learning.

The energy and the goodness of the essential learning between Zayd and Bernardine is that it's situated fundamentally in joy and trust and love. The learner—each of them in this instance—is becoming confident in the expectation that the other is reliable and responsible and that a developing faith in the other will remain steady. Tomorrow's learning will build on today's learning, which will itself lead to new learning in the future. Recognition and faith affirmed in the other generates new recognition and faith in oneself. The mother day by day is gaining assurance in her own ability to be a good mother, and the baby is becoming more self-assured as well, increasingly certain of being heard and understood. Each is supporting the other in respecting and trusting—the other person as well as oneself. The belief that they can know or discover their own deepest needs becomes self-fulfilling and begins to accelerate, leading rapidly onward—they listen more carefully to their own minds, bodies, spirits, and emotions as critical guides to future learning.

Step forward a few months or years. Look at a toddler now negotiating her apartment or a nearby park or beach or street; all five senses are fully deployed, every discovery considered and touched and smelled and—oops!—into the mouth for a taste! And soon she is sorting and building, drawing on paper or walls if the materials are at hand, imagining stories and inventing words, and putting her hand prints on everything in reach. She is a striver, looking outward toward a broader base of affiliation and relationship, asserting her blooming independence, tentatively at times and in full eruption whenever she deems it necessary—"No!" she says, a powerful new word asserting identity, power, and agency—always learning and living.

Move ahead another few years to the wonders of adolescence, a time of uncontrollable and disruptive physical changes at the onset of puberty, and of sweeping interior changes all along the way. Teenagers are the risk-takers, too often pathologized and cast in an exclusively negative light in popular culture (and in the sneering judgments of too many adults with self-justifying amnesia regarding their own younger selves), but especially in the criminal justice system and in schools that act as adjuncts or enforcers, and most pointedly when the youth in question are young men (and increasingly young women) of color. In reality, the willingness of young people to be adventurous and try new things, to take chances, and to search out a space for themselves is a force that propels youth forward. Learning anything for the first time is a risky business: riding a bike, calculating the time and distance home from school, swimming in the deep end, spelling your name, reading a book, writing a poem, learning a language. The adult job is to rig and secure the safety net; and that means, among other things, offering a cornucopia of materials and a fat catalog of experiences that will enable each child to find areas of interest and passionate engagement, allowing no one to be made to feel a complete failure, entirely inadequate and unsuccessful. After all, the best preparation for the inevitable challenges and disappointments that life brings to each of us is a long string of positive and recognized accomplishments.

And there's more, for the children we get are never exactly the children we'd expected or planned for, and as they grow into themselves, the reality of who each is becoming can contrast or conflict with our assumptions about children and our own memories of childhood, our hard-wired habits and "commonsense" values. Teachers and parents are then compelled to rethink their expectations and recalibrate their assumptions—and this is where the practice and power of that early dialogue reasserts itself as absolutely essential. The joys, inspirations, and challenges teachers and parents face every step of the way are deeply tied to the never-ending surprises these young creatures present as they become uniquely themselves rather than prestamped miniversions of us. Seeing them as they are and listening to what they have to tell us, recognizing them and delighting in their distinctiveness, embracing them through their idiosyncratic and dynamic pathways—this is the task and trial for all of us, and this is a big piece of the safety net.

There's sadness and loss involved in saying goodbye to childhood—teenage moodiness and depression is way beyond willful—but a rambunctious, trembling excitement, too, at asserting greater independence, discovering new relationships and groups, and claiming a different kind of agency and freedom. The in-between can be intermittently confusing and exhilarating: there's no turning back, so onward and upward, pushing toward the light; but there's no moving forward happily into the unknown future or that dim and anemic space the adult world seems to offer. The contradiction can be excruciating, and it surely demands question-asking and experimentation, resistance and invention, rebellion and originality.

Every young person comes to school a full human being, a collection of unique and shared experiences, a mass of contradictions and desires and dreams, and a gathering point of knowledge; each deserves, but is rarely granted, the same basic human rights as everyone else. Young people bring culture and family and language into the classroom with them, and they are acutely aware of being citizens of a world that does not yet exist—even when they stumble as they try to express that plain truth. We should never doubt it, and never forget it.

Children ask the world of us. Each child arrives in the classroom as an unruly spark of meaning-making energy on a voyage of discovery and surprise, each one a question mark and an exclamation point. Their main work, as they intuitively grasp it, is the construction not only of a life, but of an entire universe. Every school, every classroom, and every teacher must choose whether to support and aid in that construction, whether to help unbolt that energy and simultaneously open up the vitality of the universe, or to subdue and coerce their bodies and standardize their expressions while mystifying and obscuring our shared world. Every teacher must decide whether to trust students and approach them honestly as full and equal human beings with agency and capacity, with experiences and hopes and ideas that must be taken into account, or to assume that they are savages to be broken and tamed, their minds conquered and colonized. Every school person must choose whether to keep the questions and the passions alive—creating environments for exploration, for doing and making, for experimenting and hypothesizing and failing and succeeding—or to hammer the children into shape so that they leave the classroom, no longer as vital question marks and exclamation points, but as dull periods.

◇   ◇   ◇

The challenging intellectual and ethical work of teaching pivots on our ability to experience ourselves as actors and participants in a complex, dynamic, and forward-moving world—a world to explore and discover, to reimagine and to shape—and, simultaneously, to be wide-awake to the complex mixture of students who appear before us each day, young people who come to us filled with expectation and aspiration. In each direction we find fire and ice, pleasure and pain, surprise, ecstasy, and agony.

Our world: already up and running, churning and spinning and careening onward, filled with undeserved suffering and unnecessary pain on the one hand, breathtaking beauty and enduring potential on the other. And our students: each a work in progress, much like ourselves, with hopes and dreams, aspirations, skills, and capacities; with minds and hearts and spirits; with embodied experiences, histories, and stories to tell of a past and a possible future; with families, neighborhoods, cultural surrounds, and language communities all entangled and interacting to make them unique. Our students are those unruly sparks of meaning-making energy, and they are making their wobbly ways as best they can into a wild world, on a voyage of discovery and surprise.

Schools can choose to foreground the foundational qualities that promote trust and confidence, curiosity and imagination, self-direction and internal motivation—after all without any bribes or threats or stars or grades whatsoever, we arrive on these classroom shores having already learned for the most part to nurse and to eat, then to babble and talk, creep and crawl and walk, and to engage in thousands of other complex skills and undertakings. Long before the schoolhouse door presents itself we've been motivated by enthusiasm that springs from within, the deep innate human yearning to learn and to live, to experiment, to question and find out. If learning and living, constant growth and permanent development are our natural makeup, we can sensibly reject a regime of external and distant prods and stimulations in favor of what's already there—in abundance. We might as well start just from what we are.

When we respect a child or a student and support her or him in the essential work of unfolding what is within and creating a unique and specific identity, the signals of what to do and how to respond come from specific encounters with unique persons—complex, dynamic, ambiguous, twisty and wiggly—and not some disembodied, one-size-fits-all rule or principle. This stance inspires an ethic of care and a sense of reverence and awe in teachers.

Each of us is the one and only who will ever walk the earth, each of us is of infinite and incalculable value, and each is living a unique, unduplicable life in ways that must be somehow recognized and respected. Paradoxically, each of us is also exactly like everyone else in the sense that each of us is one of the many, sharing a deep human culture and experience, living and loving and learning in that brief crack of light between the infinite darkness that preceded us and the vastness that will eventually swallow us all. We participate, that is—alone and together—in the human predicament: We are born, and each of us will die by and by. But between the opening and the inevitable close, we create.

Teachers who acknowledge this evident but contradictory reality—each student who comes through that door is the one of one, and each is also a member of the same family, the common tribe—will never be running on automatic pilot, never completely satisfied or at ease. The contradiction is ultimately irresolvable, and it requires, then, constant attention and alteration, refinement and repair. The classroom is a living organism with a heart and a brain and lungs for breathing—good teachers build flexibility and openness into their work, allowing for individual curiosity and shared inquiry, singular creativity and collective expression, diversity and idiosyncrasy side by side with group work and collective action.

Our project is to unleash the human mind and spirit rather than search for techniques that will cast us as circumscribed predictors of what cannot be authentically predicted, or authorities who try to force obedience and conformity on what can never be completely contained. Humanity leaks out and moves on no matter what—humanity asserts itself.

Teaching requires teachers to let go, to get out of the way—to *let learn*. That's another contradiction to understand and work with rather than a feature to fear or flee from. After all, human beings are built on contradiction. Contradiction is fundamental to our experience and indispensable in any project of real learning.

Learning powered by contradiction takes us reeling down uncharted paths toward dissonance and destabilization that loom up whenever we are genuinely puzzled or challenged. Part of the mystery of growing up lies in the fact that learning is rarely just about new information; it's about letting go of what we think we already know. To learn means admitting at some level that you don't know, or didn't know, and therefore what you know now is itself likely contingent, partial, subject to further interrogation and discovery. You become vulnerable. And often our most transformative experiences in learning come from unexpected teachers and from facing our vulnerability—like that newborn baby.

◇   ◇   ◇

This is also what we are: distinct creatures of the imaginary. We alone among living things are able to recognize and consider that standing directly next to the world *as such* is a possible world, a world that could be or should be, but is not yet. The distance between the given world—the hard edges, the taken-for-granted, the commonplace—and those possible worlds is the territory of art and imagination, philosophy and religion, and every claim to morality.

This capacity to perceive possibility, to wonder and wander, is its own powerful engine for change and the very heartbeat of curiosity and imagination: This is the way it's always been—or this problem has bedeviled us forever—but I wonder . . . Off we go—down the rabbit hole or up into orbit—on one of life's restless and relentless journeys, exploring and experimenting, turning and spinning, inventing and adapting, chasing the irresistible human desire to know more and understand more, to see more in order to do more.

Copernicus and Galileo reimagined the cosmos, the movements of the heavenly bodies and the revolutions of the sun and the earth, while Harriet Tubman foresaw a revolution of a different type—the abolition of human bondage—and challenged the slavocracy at its base with a single-minded effort. Virginia Woolf dreamt of a room of her own, announcing that everything old was to be immediately put on trial. John Coltrane heard free jazz—devout and large—inside his head long before it burst through his horn and into our consciousness, while Dizzy Gillespie insisted on playing every note loud, "especially the wrong ones." Albert Einstein grasped relativity and then reached for world peace, and Martin Luther King Jr. aspired to a gentle revolution and a beloved community where all people—in his mind equals before God—would become equals before one another and the law. Each began with a radical dream that pushed beyond the obvious and the settled—the world as such—and flew high on the wings of that simple phrase: I wonder.

We are creatures of a living, unfolding history, spinning and turning and making our way as best we can through the vortex, squarely in the middle of things. What we do or don't do, how we choose to see the world and participate, will define us.

Seeing the world as if it could be otherwise creates yearning and liberates desire—we are freed (or condemned) to run riot. Wonder—subversive, unruly, and disruptive—challenges the current state of affairs simply by opening us up to consider alternatives. Learning to question, to interrogate, to experiment, to marvel and to wander, to construct and create—this is the foundation of lives of purpose for free people.

◇   ◇   ◇

In her autobiography *Under My Skin,* Doris Lessing (1995) provides a view of what she discovered as a child unleashed to be a learning, stretching, sometimes failing but regularly supported youngster participating in her family and her larger community. By the time she left home as a young woman, she notes that she knew:

> how to set a hen, look after chickens and rabbits, worm dogs and cats, pan for gold, take samples from reefs, cook, sew, use the milk separator and churn butter, go down a mine shaft in a bucket, make cream cheese and ginger beer, paint stenciled patterns on materials, make papier-mâché, walk on stilts made from poles cut in the bush, drive the car, shoot pigeons and guineafowl for the pot, preserve eggs—and a lot else. . . . That is real happiness, a child's happiness: being enabled

to do and to make, above all to know you are contributing to the family, you are valuable and valued. (p.103)

To do and to make, to know you are a valuable and valued part of a community and a world: this is what we are, and here is where teaching can be set powerfully into motion; here is where the essential building blocks for a lifetime of productive learning can be secured; here is where education toward freedom can begin to take hold. Learning—this unpredictable and volatile energy force located in a human world but propelled from within and intent on exploration and growth—can be nourished as it's unhooked from convention or any linear expectations whatsoever.

This, then, is what we are: unruly sparks of meaning-making energy, curious question-askers and insistent problem-solvers, intrepid explorers and restless seekers, pilgrims on a voyage of discovery and surprise—learning beings, social beings, ethical beings. Let's hold onto this sense of who and what we are—lively, beautiful, messy, contradictory, wildly diverse human beings—as we move toward imagining the schools as they could or should be, schools that might embrace that vast and vivid kaleidoscope of humanity, the schools young people ought to be able to claim as birthright.

FOUR

◇◇◇◇◇◇◇◇◇◇◇◇◇◇◇◇◇◇◇◇◇◇◇◇◇◇◇◇◇◇◇

Where are we going? I'm not too sure, but we're certainly going somewhere. We're in the mix and on the move. Perhaps we all feel appropriately a bit like the bewildered Alice stuck at the crossroads in Wonderland, famously asking directions of the Cheshire Cat: "Would you tell me, please, which way I ought to go from here?"

"That depends a good deal on where you want to get to," said the Cat.

"I don't much care where—" said Alice.

"Then it doesn't matter which way you go," said the Cat.

"—so long as I get *somewhere*," Alice added as an explanation.

"Oh, you're sure to do that," said the Cat, "if you only walk long enough."

Unlike Alice, we teachers and parents care deeply about where we're going—we are the shepherds of the dreams of others, the midwives of a kaleidoscope of possible futures—and it matters a lot; we're sure to get *somewhere*, of course, but the *where* is important to us. Will it be a place of more joy and more love, or less? Will it be a society of peace and greater participatory democracy, of more robust justice and an expanded sense of freedom? Will it be a place fit for all of our children?

I remember years ago asking Albie Sachs, the freedom fighter who later became a justice in the Constitutional Court of the new South Africa, why he and his fellow revolutionaries felt it necessary to continually spend precious time trying to articulate their plans for the post-apartheid society they hoped to build, even while victory was only a distant dream, and fighting the racist regime so immediate and so urgent. Albie answered that even though life and struggle were way too random for accurate predictions, and even though the future was unknowable, the ongoing exercise of imagining a world of fairness and equality, truth and reconciliation helped set the agenda for their work in the present. They resisted drawing a detailed map—every feature thoroughly determined in advance, every aspect precisely described, every step dogmatically designed—but sketched instead the broad outlines of a better world. It motivated them, he said, for the hard work of the moment; it focused their efforts and kept them on track; it steered them away from dead-end strategies or misguided and destructive tactics. They were citizens of a country that did not yet exist, and they wanted the new world to become increasingly visible, even in the harsh light of a life-and-death struggle. Thinking about tomorrow helped them become better actors today.

Spending some time and energy on the dream—on what we're fighting for—will surely help us, too, no matter how grand or small our struggles may be. Where are we going?

◇   ◇   ◇

I picked up a foundation report recently bearing, as I remember it, the lofty title *Building 21st Century Schools/Creating the Global Citizens of Tomorrow*, and checked out how one large prestigious national foundation was thinking about where we're going. What were its utopian dreams, I wondered, and what did they think was worth fighting for.

The authors were positively giddy about the testing and sorting regime now in place, as well as the vast potential of market-based reforms to become a handy club to crush the Indians or the Chinese. That struck me as slightly anti-utopian—dystopian, really—but I plunged ahead. Reading their economic forecasts and fanciful job projections was—surprise!—brutally boring and a little depressing. I want utopians to fly above the clouds, up toward the heavens, lifting my horizons as well as my spirits as they go, but these foundation folks seemed hopelessly lost in the weeds.

My thoughts wandered to our wondrous, wiggly, energetic, dazzling, curious, questioning, chattering, exploring, surprising, full-tilt 3-year-old grandson—what the foundation coolly refers to as a "global citizen of tomorrow." This particular little GCoT attends a lovely, slightly shabby-looking preschool that sparkles with energy and positive relationships between caregivers and kids, and among the children themselves. He loves his little school: the sand and the water, the garden and the climbing gear, the blocks and the balls and the books. Mostly he loves being with Andrew and Sadie, Elisheva and Idries, and all the other pint-sized GCoTs. He and most of his group will graduate high school in 2030.

What will the world be like for him and his wee friends at that point? What will they need to know and be able to do to live fully and purposefully? What meaning perspectives will they hold and develop along the way? What "measurable outcomes" will prepare them to dive into the wreckage of the 21st century with hope and energy?

I've got no idea, and neither does anyone else—not the self-styled think tanks cranking out their immodest reports on the future of this or that, and certainly not that self-assured foundation.

OK, wait. I do have one idea: I'd recommend that our grandson and his pals store water.

I'm kidding (kind of), but seriously, the challenges, problems, and opportunities they'll face are a blizzard of possibilities, way beyond reach. Specific job-and-skills-training projections seem feeble and silly. The changes we've seen in the last two decades alone have been breathtaking, and the rate of change is accelerating day by day.

Old folks and digital immigrants like myself share a common experience: Whenever one of us asks another for advice on an application or a computer challenge, the response is always, "Ask a 10-year-old." I've learned by now that the first answer a 10-year-old offers is, "You can Google that." I'm now in the habit of Googling first, and then asking that 10-year-old.

Adults teach computer classes in high schools across the country even though most of the time the kids are out in front of their teachers. It's like when my mom—who grew up before automobiles were common—set out to teach me to drive, and she began, "Now this is a large machine called a car; these are its keys." I lacked experience for sure, and a few lessons weren't a bad idea in my case, but I felt like snatching the keys from her, jumping into the driver's seat, and taking off. I resisted—that rebel act might have confirmed that more than once I'd snuck out late at night with a friend and gone joy-riding in her car—but cars and phones and TVs were part of my everyday landscape, nothing distant or difficult for me there. Cell phones, videos, chatting and texting, FaceTime and Instagram were innovative not so long ago, too, but no more. And so it is in schools where the curriculum too often trails after the dynamic knowledge and propulsive activity, the restless agency and insurgent gestures of the young themselves.

Getting over the delusional urge to prescribe a set of skills for ready use in 2030 or 2040 or 2050 can actually liberate us and encourage us to foreground and emphasize those things that will likely serve all of us right now, as well as 50 years from now. Far more than obedience and conformity, more than any bloodless version of "the basics" or any flattened sense of "skills," stand dispositions of mind like initiative and courage, creativity and imagination, respect for oneself and the full humanity of others, inventiveness, self-confidence and compassion, curiosity and a risk-taking, experimental spirit. These are the true basics for an education of value; these are the real skills we desperately need now—and always.

And while these are qualities that school people can never adequately teach in a didactic way—and I'll say more on this directly—they are nonetheless essential. Teachers can search for ways to nourish them, encourage and practice them, recognize and represent, display and model them—and not only in the art room (when students are lucky enough to have one) but throughout the environment and the curriculum.

Uncertain of precisely where we're going, I'm confident that these qualities and dispositions will count.

The Garden of Eden, nirvana, heaven—utopias of innocent joy and pure delight—stand side by side with images of agony, torment, unending misery, and the nightmare of hell. The sunny utopians—Thomas More, Saint-Simon, Robert Owen, Edward Bellamy, and I'll add my mother, bless her heart—with their projection of heaven on earth are worthwhile, and I'll come to a couple of them soon, but the frightening tales of their darker dystopian cousins, such as *V for Vendetta* or *Blindness,* strike somehow closer to home.

In Ray Bradbury's *Fahrenheit 451*, for example, the fire department's major activity is, astonishingly, burning books. Whenever a stash of hidden books is uncovered, sirens sound and the trucks are on their way. The remarkable explanation for why they undertake their nasty work comes from the fire chief, Captain Beatty, who points out that the people themselves have demanded that the books be burned, because books with their "great welter of nouns and verbs and adjectives" make a simple world much too complicated to enjoy. Complexity and contradiction, recognition of diversity, mutuality and compromise and dialogue—all the basics of life as it is—are the enemies of Bradbury's nightmare society as well as every other fundamentalism on earth. Keep it simple, mindless, safe. Schools in these places teach amnesia, compliance, know-nothingism. They demand obedience and loyalty to a dinky, one-dimensional picture of life—no questions please, no "great welter" of words. And yet, in a free society that's precisely what's needed—historical memory, complexity, great welters of words, and questions, always questions and more questions, questions upon questions.

The contrasting visions of terrifying totalitarianism conjured up in the furnaces of the 20th century by George Orwell and Aldous Huxley stand as horrifying projections of the charming and colorfully dressed devil beckoning from a road just up ahead and leading to a not-so-distant damnation.

The crucial differences in their visions reveal an alarming likeness of results: Orwell's *1984* is a society where free thought and speech are suppressed and books banned; he warned of a police state and a massive secret security apparatus with eyes and ears everywhere. Huxley's *Brave New World*, on the other hand, is peopled with creatures who can say or read whatever they please but who have absolutely nothing to say and no desire to read or study or wonder—with their full stomachs, uncomplicated and easily available sex, and ready drugs, they are all too busy "being free" and "having the most wonderful time" to have a thought in their heads; the population is constantly diverted by scandal, idle gossip, and consumption, and finds no use for evidence or reason whatsoever. In one dreadful society, amnesia—the forced or clever erasure of memory, history, and culture—is achieved through the wide distribution of "soma" and the "feelies" with everyone seduced and submissive; in the other, residents are beaten into submission and laid low through torture and intimidation. But in both, the results are the same: compliance, conformity, political paralysis, and complete obedience.

◇   ◇   ◇

The utopian dreamers in education have other, more hopeful and expansive plans, and they've been plugging along forever, creating unorthodox options—sometimes theoretically, but more often in specific times and concrete spaces—responding to massive social changes and real upheaval: free schools, alternative schools, the "modern school," anarchist schools and Socialist Sunday Schools, Freedom Schools and Black Panther Party Schools, Fanny Coppin and W.E.B. DuBois, Rousseau and Froebel and Steiner and Montessori, Lucy Sprague Mitchell and Caroline Pratt. Each iteration offers unique insights and charming idiosyncrasies, but there are common edges—as you'll see—among all of these little school experiments and insurgencies, and I'll pull those themes together further on.

For example, Sebastian Faure began his adult life as a priest in France but eventually broke with the church and became a teacher and an anarchist, founder of La Ruche—the Beehive—a school in a rural village set up for children of the desperately poor. The school was based on harmony and love, reflecting Faure's abiding belief in the innate goodness of children. Faure was confident that in his little school "understanding will replace duty; confidence, fear; and affection, sternness"; and he was sure that the Beehive would be a model for others to follow. The Beehive released the child from all forms of imposed discipline and coercion, and visitors reported seeing free groupings of children and adults poring over a story or puzzling through a problem. Everyone had access to work in the gardens, the fields, or the workshops, and the "hand-painted wallpaper in the dormitory and class-rooms, picturing the life of plants, flowers, birds, and animals, had a more quickening effect on the imagination of the children than any 'regular' lessons."

In Spain, Francisco Ferrer founded 109 "modern schools" between 1901 and 1909 as an attempt to fight for the child against its
enemies, to "free the child from superstition and bigotry, from the
darkness of dogma and authority." He stormed noisily and forcefully against the church as well as the state, and those powers took
note, and eventually exacted a revenge: He was persecuted for
many years, and when he was shot for his anarchist activities, his
last words were, "Long live the Modern School."

One of the best known educational insurgents of the 20th century was A. S. Neill who founded the Summerhill School in England
in the early 1920s, a school I admired and based much of my own
early work on when I began teaching decades later. Neill (1992)
hoped "to make the school fit the child" (p. 9)—instead of demanding that each child fit the established school as it was. This idea contained within it a withering criticism of the status quo, the existing
schools all around whose main business seemed, to Neill at least, to
be bending and breaking children, hammering them until they fit
as cogs in a mindlessly menacing machine, automatons without the
ability to think clearly or feel deeply. Why the steady focus on the
curriculum, the lessons, the subjects, he asked. Why the obsession
with punishments and rewards, discipline and management, order
and timetables? Why the forceful imposition of standardized ways
of seeing and knowing?

If the schools aimed to train a nation of sheep, Neill maintained,
they were doing a damn good job of it, but the negative social implications would be vast—increasing violence, greed and exploitation unchecked, selfishness and narcissism, despotism, endless war
and resurgent fascism, "a society . . . carried on the shoulders of the
scared little man" (p. 15). Neill worried that in a broad sense the
schools were foregrounding our worst qualities, things like hierar-
chical judgments, indifference, emotional and intellectual depen-
dency, provisional self-esteem, and the need to submit to certified
authority. After all, what is the deeper lesson behind report cards,
grades, and the endless batteries of tests that play the part of au-
topsies rather than diagnostics? Don't trust yourself; seek approval
from your betters. What is the point of the established schedule and
the set periods (50 minutes each for English, Biology, Study Hall,

P.E., and History, say), the exhaustive use of time, the uniform desks all in a row? You are not important; be malleable and productive in terms established by some invisible higher authority. Summerhill was engaged, then, as a site of utopian resistance.

Neill believed that the chief function of many schools is "to kill the life of children," to make them docile and obedient. "Would millions of free men allow themselves to be sacrificed to causes they had no interest in and did not understand?" he asked. "Is the future of humanity one of slaves ruled by an elite of powerful masters?" (p. 259).

Make the school fit the child—that was central to Neill's utopian vision. Don't force the child to fit the aspirations of anxious parents, the GNP or the military-industrial complex, some authorized lockstep course of study, or the existing hierarchies of race and class.

Think about what a school might look like if it were designed to fit the child. And think about who "the child" is beyond stereotypes or cardboard cutouts, beyond cartoon characters or bloodless generalizations. Surely the school would be generously supported, abundant with resources and materials of all kinds. It would be wildly idiosyncratic and rich with diversity—children of every imaginable status and background playing and working, dreaming and studying side by side—and so there would have to be multiple entry points to learning, and thousands of pathways to pursue. It would be a dynamic and restless place, never satisfied, never finished, but always engaged in the wide, wide world and always a work in progress. It would be small so that relationships could flourish and participatory democracy could be enacted, practiced, and embodied. It would be a workshop for discovery and surprise, a laboratory for inquiry and experimentation. And the curriculum would unfold in endless pursuit of an inexhaustible question: What knowledge and experience is of most value?

◇   ◇   ◇

My friend and colleague Bill Schubert—popularizer of what he calls the "basic curriculum question" (What knowledge and experience is of most value?), and eccentric dream-catcher in his own right—is a John Dewey scholar, and he's studied the eminent philosopher's canon from top to bottom. Bill first introduced me to one of his favorite Dewey pieces, a little-known gem called "Dewey Outlines Utopian Schools" that was published as an op-ed in the *New York Times* in 1933. In it Dewey imagines time-traveling to a future Utopia, visiting the "schools" and speaking with the Utopians about education. Schubert wrote an entire book called *Love, Justice, and Education* (2010) dissecting and analyzing every sentence of Dewey's little travelogue, and that wondrous meditation, too, is worth a special trip.

Dewey opens with this provocative observation: "The most Utopian thing in Utopia is that there are no schools at all." It seems that in Utopia educating the young involves simply engaging them and immersing them as fully as possible into every aspect of the life of the community. They learn everything by doing everything.

As in the everyday schools we know, children do gather together regularly with more mature people, but they convene on large grounds with working gardens and orchards and greenhouses, and these gathering places are like spacious homes with shops attached for wood-and-iron-working and for making textiles. There are no more than 200 students at any meeting place, since that seems to the Utopians to be the limit of intimate acquaintance. There are no desks in rows, no teachers standing front and center. There are books everywhere as well as a well-stocked central library, and there are small museums and scientific laboratories round and about. Children's interests are honored and built upon, and they move naturally to what draws them, and then on to the next thing and the next. Children and youth act often as we might imagine apprentices to act, that is, they observe, participating in simpler operations at first, and develop greater skills and more independence as they grow and go along.

When Dewey asks his new friends about objectives and purposes it takes quite a lengthy effort for them to wrap their minds around what he's trying to get at—it seems to them quite a bizarre question. The whole notion of objectives and purposes apart from life and work is alien and unnecessary, and they have trouble taking it seriously. They explain to Dewey that asking about objectives is like asking them why children should live at all: "of course, we . . . try to make their lives worthwhile to them; of course, we try to see that they really do grow, that they really develop." But any objective beyond developing life seems ridiculous at best.

Again, when Dewey pushes on and inquires about how the Utopians would know, then, if young people were acquiring the necessary knowledge to function fully and well in society, he's met with blank looks. How, they wonder, would it be possible in the vast majority of cases for young people *not* to learn what they needed to know? How could they avoid learning if they were living? Yes, Dewey agrees, but how do you know they are learning what you want them to learn? The Utopians are amused and they tease their visitor: Are there external examiners in your schools to certify that the little ones can walk or talk? Are the infants and toddlers tested to be absolutely sure? Are grades entered into their permanent records?

The Utopians speculate that in Dewey's time an economic/social system based on personal acquisition and private possession must have become so dominant that everything—even something as natural as learning—was recast as a part of a vast and all-encompassing acquisitive system with its hallmarks of rivalry, competition, external rewards and punishments, sorting examinations and structures of promotion. Education could never be enjoyable in itself in that system, they thought; "enjoyment" under such a rigid and rigorous administration must have necessarily been suppressed, deferred, or redirected.

When Dewey, knowing now that the Utopians reject the acquisition of skills or information as a worthy goal, asks what *attitudes*, then, are the most important ones to develop, they again resist any sort of ranking, stating that the all-around development of the young is what's important. Dewey accepts this, but feels that he can nonetheless see that for the Utopians developing a sense of empowerment, a sense of positive power, is a central value, and that it involves the "elimination of fear, of embarrassment, of constraint, of self-consciousness; eliminated the conditions which created the feeling of failure and incapacity. Possibly it included the development of a confidence, of readiness to tackle difficulties, of actual eagerness to seek problems instead of dreading them and running away from them. It included a rather ardent faith in [human capacity]."

◇   ◇   ◇

Let's take Dewey, Neill, and all the other insurgents along with us as we wind our twisty ways toward tomorrow's freedom dreams, diving ever deeper into our own imaginations and wondering together about the kinds of schools we want and need, the schools we will joyously promote and courageously fight for today. And let's be crystal clear that these schools are not designed for the few—the privileged or the lucky or the elite, the intellectually "gifted" or the especially talented—but for the many, based on a fundamental guiding principle, that all children have the right to a generously supported free, public neighborhood/community school whose efforts are directed to the full development of each and of all. The utopians have jump-started our efforts, offering us three ginormous points of departure to embrace and build upon, so I'll start there. The schools we'll struggle to create, the schools all students deserve, will:

1. **Display an ardent faith in human agency—in individual as well as collective capacity** (Dewey and others)

2. **Fit (or align to) the children in their infinite and dynamic diversity—not the other way round** (Neil and others)

3. **Embrace learning as the identical twin of living** (Faure and others)

Let's all of us—students and families, teachers and educators, members of our varied and diverse communities—keep pushing and building our vision of schools as they could be, and perhaps should be, in abundance. Let's get the ideas flowing, let's work toward articulating a shared dream, and let's develop a more complete inventory. I'll add a dozen and a half more in the rest of this chapter. But that is not the end of it.

4. Perform freedom

The schools we deserve will encourage students to perform freedom, to become the authors of their own scripts, the architects of their own identities, and central actors in their own dramas. And those schools will not only nourish and support children and youth in the essential work of constructing minds of their own, but will help them become world citizens capable of seeking justice, defending the weak, standing up against wrongdoing and violations of human rights, and defying all brutal or undemocratic authority.

Freedom, of course, is never a strictly individual pursuit, and it can never mean absolute autonomy—you can't will yourself to be or to do anything you feel like being or doing. I can't, for example, magically become the starting short-stop for the Chicago Cubs, even though I want to. Maybe a backup, well, that's not likely either, so maybe I'll just have to pass on that dream. Nor am I free to go stomping through the world without regard to anyone else. Freedom is social; it's found in the company of others.

We are each thrust—sometimes gently, often rudely—into a peopled and ongoing world. We each emerge at a specific time and place, into a society already up and running, steadily charging forward, and that received world is obviously not of our choosing. We must somehow choose ourselves against the rough surfaces and the hard facts as we find them. We must *choose* who to be in a world we did not choose—we must decide what to make out of the raw materials with which we've been made.

Freedom is sought within and against the high walls of facticity, the landscape that's already there; freedom points to the practice of looking at those walls through your own eyes, of thinking and rethinking what to make of them, of locating yourself within community and naming those walls as barriers to your (or your neighbor's) development as a free human being. Freedom, then, is an invitation and impulse to act against imposed impediments, rather than some fairy dust sprinkled on inert and insecure beings, cowed or controlled young people as they shuffle out of boot camp; it's more than a gift from a higher power—bestowed, received, accepted.

Freedom is only brought to life as action against imposed restrictions, as movement against "un-freedom."

We need spaces where young people can be supported and encouraged as they reach toward freedom and as they develop the fundamental and basic characteristics of free people, that is, as they grow into the arts of liberty: initiative, questioning, courage, audacity, imagination, creativity, inventiveness, empathy and fellow feeling, respect for self and others, compassion and love, self-confidence, curiosity, and risk-taking. These are the attributes of spirit that delineate a free and enlightened people; these are the qualities of heart that can move things forward; these are the dispositions of mind that can challenge cynicism and easy resignation with hope. And yet none of these things can be taught frontally from the top down, and none can be learned passively. Rather they must be modeled and supported, encouraged and accommodated, defended and displayed, and mostly practiced again and again and again.

In my classroom many years ago we delighted in a kind of preschool patois constantly being invented and reinvented by the kids but quickly incorporated into the culture of the place—words like *snow blurries* (sudden snow bursts) and *Africot* (half a peach, half a plum, such a fruit!). We also all spoke a fun and sometimes funny feminist argot: *firefighter, flight attendant, cowhand, waitron!* Our block area had, we thought, the biggest collection of multicultural and stereotype-challenging wedgies ever assembled: a Black male nurse and a Chicana doctor, an Asian female cop and an African business person—on and on and on.

One day we went on a field trip to our local firehouse. A young recruit showed us around, letting kids try on the big hats, ring the bell, and sit in the front seat of the engine. It was totally awesome, until a 4-year-old girl asked our new friend, "So, when are you going to get a woman firefighter here?" The fireman exploded in mocking laughter. "A woman!" he cried. "I hope never! The neighborhood would burn to the ground! This is no place for women."

Wait? What? Why did he say that mean thing? Back at school the child dictated a letter to the mayor about getting a woman firefighter up in our neighborhood: "It's not fair," she declared indignantly. And she concluded emphatically, "Women can do any-thing!" She was experiencing and exercising freedom in action—lessons for a lifetime.

In that little room we wanted to make a wide and deep space for every child to find pathways to a life lived with courage, hope, and love, a life worth doing, and so the place was always a work in progress. We read the story of Rosa Parks each year on December 1, acted out the drama, sang Freedom Songs, and wore kid-made, silk-screened T-shirts with Rosa's image behind bars. We wanted the kids to feel that they and their families could stand up in acts of repair and hope, that something could always be done, no matter what.

We could never have anticipated what happened one morning when a mom dropping off her 3-year-old told us that she'd just learned that she'd been laid off from her job as a nurse in a public hospital slated to be shuttered for budgetary reasons. Her spirits were down, but she was planning to attend a community rally that evening. Next day her spark had returned and she was on a freedom high: "The whole community is up in arms," she told us. "They rely on that hospital, and they care about us." The rally had been huge, filled with spirit and singing and determination.

Each day she brought news from the hospital, and her accounts became a wildly anticipated and vivid "chapter book" shared at morning circle. She animated her stories with a colorful cast of characters—nurses and friends, community activists and ordinary folks—in a Dickensian slog through the city, and she was in the thick of it, eye-witness reporter, participant-observer, hero, sage, mom, and friend.

When the workers and community members occupied the hospital to keep it open, the kids were excited because, like Rosa Parks, they would not be moved. And when they escalated by announcing a hunger strike, the kids were electrified: "When will they eat?" "Are they sad?"

"Let's bring them something to eat," one five-year-old suggested at snack time that day. Good idea! We baked two big carrot cakes and decorated each with hearts and stars. And next morning, right after circle, we took a field trip to bring carrot cake to the hunger-strikers—missing the concept, perhaps, but wholly aligned with the spirit of the struggle. This was the practice of freedom.

The freedom we celebrate, the freedom we often take for granted, came to life as a result of people pushing against barriers and knocking down walls—the abolitionists and the formerly enslaved runaways, labor organizers, civil rights agitators, suffragettes and feminists, sheroes and queeroes, and many, many more. The accomplishments and successes of these freedom fighters established new norms of living; looking back we can miss the uncertainty, the risk, the courage embodied in each of them. The social movements they built are vivid examples of people defining their needs and their desires against the conditions of the lives they'd inherited; each involved challenges, determined opposition and an unpredictable future; each disturbed the peace, broke the law, and, yes, finally changed the course of history. Each began in a settled and a given world, and each knocked over the apple cart as folks reached toward something new.

In the schools we need, free people, young and old, will learn to actively oppose the objectification of themselves and others, to object to being inspected, sermonized, indoctrinated, spied on, scrutinized, listed, assessed, chided and checked off, appraised, probed, admonished, and reprimanded. Everyone will engage naturally in naming the circumstances of their lives, identifying impediments to their full humanity and the humanity of others, and planning ways, in association with others, to overcome those obstacles and remake our shared world.

Paradoxically, we are never so free as when we confront a wall, and, suddenly aware of limits, develop a deeper sense of our own agency, allowing us to fight back against the forces of "un-freedom." In dissent, opposition, resistance, and rebellion we discover the most precious spaces of freedom.

5. Function democratically

Education for free people is powered by a particularly precious and fragile ideal that lies at the heart of democracy: *every human being is of infinite and incalculable value,* each the one of one, a unique intellectual, emotional, physical, spiritual, moral, and creative force. Each of us is born equal in dignity and rights, each endowed with reason and conscience and agency, each deserving, then, a dedicated place in a community of solidarity as well as a vital sense of brotherhood and sisterhood, recognition and appreciation. That basic ethic has no start date, and no discard-by date; it applies to human beings of every shape and condition and circumstance from beginning to end.

Since there is no royalty and no superior class in a functional democracy, the people with the problems must also be understood to be the people with the solutions, and the fullest development of each individual—given the tremendous range of ability and the delicious stew of race, ethnicity, points of origin, and background—is the necessary condition for the full development of the entire community; conversely, the fullest development of all is essential for the full development of each.

Democracy is not a spectator sport: The right to vote is foundational, of course, and extending and expanding the franchise against forces of restriction and suppression is critical, but voting is a means to democratic life, not democracy itself. When voting is manipulated by money and power it becomes superficial; when the choices on offer are between Tweedledee and Tweedledum they are meaningless; and when voting is no more than a formal exercise in ballot marking it loses its essential purpose. Democracy asks us to learn more and to know more in order to make wiser decisions; democracy demands participation.

Democracy encourages us to see ourselves as simultaneously the one and only and one of the many—and so we express our individuality, and we enact our solidarity. The old cautionary questions make sense: If I'm not for me, who will be? If I'm for me alone, what am I? We are looking toward the spirit of associative living, the deep culture of democracy—self-respect and respect for others, a world of one entangled in the universe of all.

When students at Berkeley High School (Berkeley, California) walked out one recent day after an incident with aggressively racist cyber graffiti, a veteran African American English teacher posted an interpretation of events:

> Today's rally . . . was pretty impressive, but I want to assure those doubters that yes, it was organized "on the fly." Of course, students in the Black Student Union . . . have developed a great deal of experience in the last couple of years. Ironically, BHS Staff were not involved in the organizing and execution of the rally and walkout. But faculty escorted students around town, led discussions in class when they returned, comforted and advised students after school. . . . The protest at its most expansive was not a protest against the school, and its policies, though it well could have been. That would have been fair. We CAN do a much better job preparing students for the world they will face, and we can create structures more responsive to the needs of students. We do this every day, but we can do it better, and we can do it smarter. . . . I would argue that students took this moment very seriously; I just hope that we can continue examining the ways we can better serve students. Business as usual was NOT EVEN POSSIBLE today. When the school agreed to get out of the way, let students express themselves, and reflect on what had happened, some significant learning occurred. I asked my final class, "What next?" Students have plenty of answers to this question. They are not organizing or marching out of class because they are lazy, undisciplined, or naive, or simply uninformed. . . . [They and we] want our school and our society to work better for us all.

This is participatory democracy in practice, one for all and all for one, everyone on the move and in the mix.

The first pedagogical gesture in authentically democratic schools is dialogue—speaking with the possibility of being heard, and listening with the expectation of being transformed in some large or small measure. The schools we deserve will offer experiences with dialogue, experiments in associative living, exercises in learning to live together, and a rich culture of recognition and profound compassion for one another and our shared world.

6. Support children and youth as they pursue their own interests

Children are human beings, not human becomings, and human beings are natural seekers, meaning-makers, and inventors—we create as expressions of our consciousness. The young child learning to speak, the older child discovering through work at the easel that red and blue mix together to become purple, the teenager producing a song or a poem or a novel bit of slang, a zine or a blog—these are all everyday instances of inventors at work, pursuing their own interests.

Youth Radio, a 2-decades-old youth development organization and independent media production space in Oakland, California, provides vibrant pathways for teenagers to pursue their own interests—to hear, to report, and to tell their own stories through audio documentaries. Youth Radio works with area high school students as well as youth who have left school.

When one Youth Radio reporter did a story on "sagging," the teen style of letting one's pants droop to precipitous levels, his friend GW offered some serious insight: It's like code-switching when you speak. He pointed out that he only speaks "Oaklandese" when talking with other folks who live in Oakland, but might switch into a more universal language when he encounters people from elsewhere. Same thing with pants—he might sag in certain areas, and in other areas pull them up so he can "infiltrate the system." GW is proudly bilingual in sagging, and he expresses his bilingualism brilliantly.

The reporter was duly impressed: "That's my man GW, dropping that knowledge."

Drop That Knowledge is the title of a dazzling book about Youth Radio (Soep & Chávez, 2010) as well as a generative idea that means recognizing and unlocking the wisdom of young people, while pointing to the power of analytical and critical thinking that folks always have the potential to engage. It offers challenges to both young people and adults—the charge to youth is to honor their own experiences and insights even as they investigate the life worlds of others; the charge to adults is to drop the patronizing pose of expertise and authority as they open their eyes and ears to the beats and the cadences of youth, and work to become students of their students.

It's wrong—inaccurate and dishonest, as well as unjust and corrupt—to assume that young people (or any other human beings) can possibly be known by their statistical profiles (age, race, income, zip code, occupation, test score) or best understood without listening systematically to how they explain themselves, how they see the world, how they constitute and construct their enthusiasms and preferences and responses, and how they pursue their own interests. In the schools we deserve, this listening, observing, attempting to see through their eyes can encourage youth to develop their own tools against propaganda, political agendas, dogma, and all manner of impositions and stereotypes. These schools and classrooms will provide children ongoing opportunities to exercise their resourcefulness and their agency, to speak up and act out, to dive into projects and performances of importance to them, to create their own styles and gestures and art and argot without domineering or patronizing responses from adults.

Like all other human beings, children and youth want to be of use—they cannot productively be treated as "objects" to be taught "subjects" and then in some far-off future spring forth as fully formed and experienced actors. Young people need community and school support as they identify and work to solve the real problems of their communities—the life of the schools we need will be in their hands.

A 6th-grade life science class in Pittsburgh made a regular practice of going outside to the field just behind the school in order to explore nature. This teacher thought it was important to join her students in regarding nature itself rather than continually indulging the abstractions of the classroom, and they usually found something beyond the lesson of the day. While looking at leaves, for example, they encountered an owl pellet which was dissected to uncover the exquisite skeleton of a doomed mouse; while examining trees on another day, they devised a way to measure the height by pacing off the sides of a right triangle.

The teacher had made an annual tradition of collecting water samples from the nearby creek, once in the fall and then again in the spring. They would do simple chemical assays on the water, looking for evidence of amoebic life, leaf mold, and heavy metals. It was easy to see that leaves were clogging the stream in the fall and were cleared by the spring rains. But they began to notice that over a few cycles the traces of metals were steadily going up and the carbon signs of life were going down. Looking over the stream assay charts from past years, a group of students asked the simple question: why?

Where were the heavy metals coming from? What had changed? This set the class off on an adventure. Every week they went out to the stream and ventured farther up, taking new samples. Then they asked the teacher to go even farther upstream, 10 and then 20 miles, tracing the stream and taking and labeling water samples every half mile. What they discovered was that the toxicity of the stream started right past a factory 12 miles away, and that the poison was not in the water above it. The students wrote a letter to the Environmental Protection Agency reporting their findings, and the factory was found out. A few years earlier they had abandoned the cost of treating their outflows and began dumping directly into this nearby stream. The factory was fined and required to clean up its act. And the mold and amoebae returned. After that, the class came to see itself as not just exploring nature, but as looking out for and protecting the earth. They became more engaged, citizens who could identify and solve real problems.

7. Tell the difficult and tangled truths

Imagine if we had been teaching or creating schools in America in the days of chattel slavery; that urgent reality, as we can easily see now, would have been informative, even foundational, in everything we undertook. That peculiar institution, even if unnoticed or unacknowledged, was a defining truth, and everyone lived in its shadow and chose whom to be and how to act in light of human bondage and chattel slavery as the central fact of social life.

Because "we've arrived safely here" 150 years later, it's easy to imagine we would have been brave truth-tellers, thoughtful and effective Abolitionists in both our classrooms and our communities. We'd have taught our students about the evils of slavery, helped organize the Underground Railroad if we were among the "free" citizenry, attempted to run away if we were one of the captive Africans, listened to and amplified the voices of the silenced, assisted Harriet Tubman on her journeys, and made common cause with Frederick Douglass and John Brown. Of course, had we done any of that, had we even spoken up against slavery, we would have been speaking against the law and the Constitution; the Supreme Court and the Founding Fathers; the Bible and the local preacher; our parents, perhaps; some neighbors and friends, certainly; and most pillars of the community. But, OK, we may as well flatter ourselves today and imagine that we'd have stood up in the tradition of resistance to injustice and fighting for freedom way back then—when it mattered.

But it always matters, and that flattery doesn't take us very far, and it settles nothing for today. We still live in shadows, and we still bend to the afterlife of slavery—mass incarceration, redlining and super-exploitation, racialized health outcomes, militarized police forces, and two-tiered school systems. Slavery was ended, but the poor descendants of Africans fill the nation's handcuffs, courtrooms, and jail cells. Other histories emerge as well, calling and challenging us: Can we acknowledge and tell the truth about our settler-colonial past and honor our commitments to Indigenous peoples today? Will we fully recognize and honor women's work? What else might we be missing now?

Most schools live on half-truths at best, and dissembling is the sad, often exhausting norm of behavior. One pervasive example is the widely dispensed notion that standardized test scores are a fair measure of student intelligence, achievement, or worth. This isn't true. An important aspect of truth-telling is asking important questions— imagine unleashing an inquiry project with youngsters at the start of testing season: Why do we take standardized tests? What do they tell us about intelligence or aptitude? Who typically does well on these tests, and who does poorly? Why do they take up so much time and space in the school? Do test scores correlate with family income or background? How are test questions determined? Is cultural bias a factor in test construction? Can test-taking be learned or coached? What assessment alternatives might be employed? Why?

This kind of inquiry could lead anywhere, and students might discover and learn a lot, some of it quirky and novel—I just learned, for example, that there are 85 billion neurons in a 3rd-grader's brain, each with over 10,000 separate connections, which made me wonder again why we talk in schools about an 8-year-old who is at the "3rd-grade level."

Students at a high school in Ohio pursued an investigation of high-stakes standardized testing as a senior project. After weeks of inquiry they issued a comprehensive report that they called "Failing the Test" and presented it at a school assembly. The report covered finances and costs, the correlation between student background and test success, the time taken from other curriculum priorities to practice and prepare for tests, an analysis of cultural bias in questions, and the profits generated by testing corporations and the test-prep industry. The report included surveys as well as in-depth interviews with students, parents, and educators. At the school assembly the student-researchers received a standing ovation from everyone, including administrators. Suddenly the all-powerful Oz-of-testing was revealed in his ordinariness.

The key lesson here is not about testing. The lesson, rather, is about curiosity and truth-seeking—it's an extended demonstration of the power of investigation and the importance of searching for difficult and tangled truths.

If we hope to become truth-tellers and ethical actors in our own society we need to make every effort to pay attention, to open our eyes again and again, and to try to sort out those things that are fair and just and beneficial for the world from those that are unjust or terrible and therefore unacceptable—even if customary, conventional, authorized, and legal; even when completely expected. Telling the truth is never automatic and rarely easy, but in the schools we need, educators will work at it every day.

8. Practice courage

Education empowers folks to challenge orthodoxy, dogma, and mindless complacency, to be skeptical of all authoritative claims, to interrogate and trouble the given and the taken-for-granted—that's why education is the enemy of every brand of tyrant. Dictators and oppressors are fearful of educated people, and they all send the same message: Be careful what you say, stay close to the official story, stick to the authorized text, stay in line, keep quiet, and keep your head down.

There's a tension inherent in kids coming to trust their own views and knowledge—learning to speak unapologetically about the experiences over which they hold authority—while noting that their views are but a piece of a complex world in which other knowledges, perspectives, and experiences are also vital. That's a central feature of successfully negotiating adolescence, and good schools can help youngsters dive into this contradiction with zest, humor, and intelligence.

A Youth Radio reporter was stopped by the transit police in a subway station on the way to a staff meeting. In a clear case of racial profiling, he was placed in handcuffs as the police questioned him about nearby robberies. "Leave me alone," he said. "This is not how you approach a citizen." As Soep and Chávez (2010) observe, "Even with handcuffs snapping around his wrists, [he] had the presence of mind to pose a question about youth citizenship." Coincidentally, a television crew was at the station and caught the confrontation on tape, but he could never get the other news media group to share their tape for his complaint. But his particular brilliance was that he was able to produce a story about the incident, including the lack of solidarity from the TV crew, and explore the implications for power, race, and youth. This was a space organized by smart educators for the enactment of agency and courage.

In Bertolt Brecht's play *Galileo* the great astronomer sets forth into a world dominated by a mighty church and an authoritarian state power: "The cities are narrow and so are the brains," he declares recklessly. Intoxicated with his own insights, Galileo finds himself propelled toward revolution. Not only did his radical discoveries about the movement of the stars free them metaphorically from the "crystal vault" that received truth insistently claimed fastened stars to the sky, but his insights suggested something even more danger-ous: that human beings, too, are embarked on a great voyage, that we too are free and without the easy support that dogma provides. That metaphor was one bridge too far, and here Galileo raised the stakes and risked taking on the establishment in the realm of its own authority—and it struck back fiercely. Forced to renounce his life's work under the exquisite pressure of the Inquisition, Galileo denounced what he knew to be true, and was welcomed back into the church and the ranks of the faithful, but exiled from humanity— by his own word. A former student confronted him in the street then: "Many on all sides followed you . . . believing that you stood, not only for a particular view of the movement of the stars, but even more for the liberty of teaching— in all fields. Not then for any particular thoughts, but for the right to think at all. Which is in dispute."

The schools and classrooms we need will defend the right of students to have minds of their own, the right to pursue an argu-ment into uncharted spaces, the right to challenge the state or the church or any conventional thinking and its orthodoxy in the pub-lic square. The right to think at all.

9. Search for root causes

The schools we deserve will be built so that participants can learn *from* the natural world, not about her; *from* history, not about it; *from* fish and farming, construction and carpentry, gardening and Gypsies, quilting and quantum mechanics—not simply about them. Being immersed in the common world creates the essential condi-tions for learning by doing: interrogating, acting, producing, in-quiring, and participating. No longer a set of tourist destinations, learning goes deeper and travels further. And most important, folks develop confidence in themselves as creators and meaning-makers in an infinite universe, not simply consumers of a static world.

Students in a New York City elementary school embarked on a study of immigration and were on their initial field trip to investigate a living site of intersection between newly arriving residents when they stopped for lunch along the banks of the Hudson River. Playing on the shore a few students started arguing about whether the river was flowing up or down, north or south. They threw sticks into the water and observed them closely, but the evidence was contradictory, and the debate heated up. Soon the entire class was looking closely at the water and trying to figure out what was puzzling to them: the river seemed to be flowing away from, rather than toward, the sea. Their smart teacher entered the discussion, not to tell them what she thought, but to keep them focused on the river itself and what the river was telling them. Eventually they returned to school, but now determined to find out why the river was behaving strangely.

A month later—following many return trips to the water's edge, map-making and art projects, charts and graphs, journeys to speak to scientists and environmental activists as far away as Spuyten Duyvil—the class knew that the Hudson was a tidal river, flowing intermittently toward and away from the sea depending on the moon. Satisfied with what the river had taught them, the class was ready to return to the immigration study.

The Exception and the Rule is one of Bertolt Brecht's "teaching plays" written around 1930. These short plays were performed in schools and factories in order to prod people to go to the root of things. The play tells the story of a rich merchant who must journey across the desert in order to complete an oil deal. The merchant is accompanied on his trip by a porter (the "Coolie") and a guide. The merchant is increasingly brutal with the Coolie, and also frightened without the police nearby to protect him. When he fires the guide, the merchant and the Coolie get lost in the desert and their water supplies run dangerously low. The Coolie comes to the merchant during the night in order to offer his remaining water, but the merchant misinterprets his action, and shoots and kills the Coolie.

In court, evidence of the murder is presented. The judge concludes that the merchant had every right to fear the Coolie and that

he was justified in shooting in self-defense regardless of whether there was an actual threat or whether the merchant merely felt
threatened. The merchant was acquitted.

The Coolie is a victim of the *rule* of wealth, while the merchant,
a proven murderer, walks away free—*the exception and the rule.*
Brecht sees that as the root of things.

Charles Darwin, Margaret Mahler, Galileo Galilei, and Karl Marx
moved things forward by interrogating the world before them,
searching for origins and essences, principles and fundamentals:
Darwin learned from nature, Mahler from children and their mothers, Galileo from the stars, and Marx from economic structures; each
discovered and explained powerful but invisible forces operating
underneath. In the schools we deserve today's little Marie Curies and
Albert Einsteins will—in large and small ways—try to move things
forward as well by plunging in and digging deeper, searching for
root causes.

10. Expect young people to become central actors in their own lives and in the larger world

The schools we need will be geared toward allowing every human
being to reach a fuller measure of her or his humanity. It's the ir-
reducible and incalculable value of every human life linked to the
work of unlocking and releasing the power of each and all that
gives education for free people its fundamental shape and direction. These schools will stand side by side with the universal human longing of various people—in different times and places, under
vastly different circumstances, using different tools and tactics—to
achieve greater freedom, fairness, equity, access, agency, recognition, openness, and sustainability. That striving posits the forces of
oppression and exploitation, racism and discrimination as unnatural human constructions—and therefore changeable. And this recognition encourages us to step into history as actors/participants as
well as observers and meaning-makers. In this way human agency
will find its rightful place at the center of the school experience.

When students at the University of Missouri, after years of organizing and months of agitation, convinced members of the storied

football team to join their demand that top administrators resign because of a continuing atmosphere of racial antagonism, the players faced a tough decision: take a huge risk of losing their scholarships and their best chance at a college education, or close their eyes to their fellow students who were reaching out to them. The student body was only 8% African American, but the football team was over 65% Black, and football had a unique place on campus, generating millions of dollars in revenue. The players met together and declared that "injustice anywhere is a threat to justice everywhere," and the entire team (including the coaching staff!) followed the lead of the African American players, declaring a strike and a determination to refuse to play. Within hours the president was gone, and the strike over.

This action was taken without any guarantees. It showed the latent power people have, and how that power becomes manifest when they organize themselves and act in unison. It demonstrated as well how an educator—the unlikely head coach in this case—can support an act of courage and open a space for reflection and action, assisting students as they step into history as major actors, This is a lasting and powerful lesson.

11. Practice cooperation

Where questioning, researching, and undertaking active work in the community is the order of the day, helping others is never a form of charity, an act that, intentionally or not, impoverishes both recipient and benefactor. Nor is it cheating; sharing knowledge, experiences, insights, skills, understandings, and perspectives is entirely natural in the schools we deserve and need. A spirit of open communication, interchange, and analysis is entirely commonplace in these spaces, as is a certain natural disorder, some anarchy and chaos, as there is in any busy workshop. But there will also be a sense of joy and a deeper discipline at work, the discipline of getting things done and learning with and from one another and through life. We see clearly, then, that education at its best is always productive and fruitful—in a way that training, for example, never can be—and that offering knowledge and learning and education to others is never a loss for oneself. Like love, learning is generative: the more you have, the better off you are; giving it away freely and generously diminishes no one, takes nothing away.

12. Choose love

The most wonderful teachers I know communicate to their students a powerful message: I know you; I love you. Sometimes kids make us laugh, sometimes they make us cry; sometimes they drive adults up a tree. But a teacher or a parent can dislike a child's actions and still love that child. In fact, for some of us, the needy child or the struggling child or the naughty child calls out to our loving instincts more strongly and more insistently than any others.

To be fully experienced, our love must be given unconditionally, not dependent on performance or compliance or even behavior—love is present and steady, not so much earned as available. This means that the implicit and unstated message—and hopefully explicitly stated whenever appropriate—even when delivered as a reprimand or a punishment, is, "Because I love you." Don't run in the street—because I love you; do your algebra—because I love you; stop fighting—because I love you. They should hear it and feel it all day long—like a soft spring rain or a ray of sunshine peeking from behind a cloud—even when implied, even if uttered through gritted teeth, even when they are being unlovable.

This cannot be a romanticized or an abstract love—valorizing children or the "authentic voices of youth" is a stance that's all but inevitable when relations with children are at a distance, or the brush with youth and youth culture is quick and breezy. Rather than heroizing the young as objects of adulation—or demonizing them as objects of fear, the opposite but similarly uninformed response—we must learn to dwell within the conflicts and contradictions that are at the heart of living and growing up, learning and teaching.

Love for our students must begin in faith and be forged in the dailiness of living our lives together. The best high school baseball coach I ever knew had a simple mantra during games—he would say softly to each player at moments of stress or expectation or failure, "I see you. No worries, I see you." It felt like love.

Children and youth can never thrive outside that circle of love. The ethical core of the schools we need must always be love—love for oneself, love for others, love for our shared world. These schools will be linked up to a fast-moving, ever-lengthening love train, roaring across the land with a message that replaces greed and repression and prejudice and hierarchy and surveillance and control with community, peace, balance, simple fairness, and love—all kinds of love for all kinds of people in every situation. The radical message is simply: teach love.

13. Resist orthodoxy by asking the next question—and the next

To catch up with the world in motion—to try to grasp and understand it, to plunge ahead as participants toward the new and the unknown—we commit ourselves to ongoing observation and steady interaction with the world. We become adventurers *in search of* the unknown rather than acting in *accordance with* or *accommodation to* the known—unsatisfied with dogma or orthodoxy, clichéd or faith-based explanations of any kind. As free people we are charged to look more deeply and to search more thoroughly. We ask questions: Why? Who benefits? What does it mean? What else?

In the schools we need, students will require no one's permission to interrogate the universe: Why? How come? What if? Wherever we are and whenever we step up and take off, we can embody the spirit of the problem-posers and the question-askers: What does it mean to be human? Who in the world am I? (and who am *I* in the world?) How did I get here and where am I going? What in the world are my choices and my chances? What does it mean to be educated? What did I learn that the teacher didn't know? What's my story, and how is it like or unlike the stories of others? What is my responsibility to those others?

Those questions and approaches are as revolutionary today in Chicago or Detroit or New Orleans or most anywhere else as they were in the Middle Ages in Europe or in apartheid South

Africa or in segregated Mississippi half a century ago. Asking the next question is an antidote to orthodoxy, a hedge against some new form of dogma following the latest discovery or insight or explanation.

There are other powerful questions that will guide the schools we need: How do students learn? What are their preferences? If they could choose, what would they do? What strengths and interests do they bring with them into this space? How could these be built upon and made into bridges toward deeper and wider ways of knowing? Could conversation about large goals and ethical purposes productively power the daily life in these schools? More than any textbook or theory, more than adherence to a specific philosophy or ideology, we invent and reinvent ourselves through questions, and students and teachers become fellow travelers and essential cocreators.

Practically anything from the lofty to the mundane can be the object of serious inquiry and provide opportunities for teachers and students to enact a curriculum that resists frozen thinking and received wisdom. When I read, for example, that in Arkansas—where Governor Huckabee had become the poster boy of dramatic weight loss and a leader in the national campaign against obesity—school report cards would include each child's BMI, body mass index, I thought, Wow! What a great opportunity for Arkansas educators!

Obesity is indeed a massive public health problem and its dimensions have been growing for decades: Obesity is the number one killer-disease in the United States, and today's children will be the first generation in history to fail to outlive their parent generation, chiefly because of fat. But rather than dully accept that the BMI notation will make students and parents more aware of the scale of the thing, smart teachers might hold the initiative up to scrutiny and interrogation.

In the interest of historicizing everything, we might ask:

♦ What is the history of obesity as a health problem in the United States and elsewhere? Is it considered an "eating disorder," and if so, how is it like/unlike other "eating disorders"? What part of the problem is genetic predisposition, what part habit or education, what part access?

◆ What is the history of engaging schools to solve broader social problems? What has been the result of mandating alcohol and drug awareness programs, for example, or suicide prevention and abstinence programs?

In the spirit of politicizing everything, we can go further:

◆ Who decided to mandate the inclusion of the BMI? Was there broad participation and dialogue by parents, students, teachers, or the wider community?
◆ What industries suffer because of obesity, and which ones benefit? What's the relationship of fat and sugar to the problem? What public and economic policies impact the sugar industry, for example?
◆ Is obesity correlated in any way to income, class, race, or gender? How?
◆ Are exercise facilities available equally across communities regardless of income or property values? Are parks equitably distributed?
◆ Are fruits and vegetables accessible equitably regardless of community income?

In the spirit of active inquiry close to home, again more questions:

◆ How much time is allotted to recess and physical education?
◆ Are all students equally encouraged or even required to participate in sports and games?
◆ What is a typical school lunch?
◆ Does the school sell soda, candy, or fatty foods from vending machines? Does it sell fast food or junk food? Fruits and vegetables? Why?
◆ Do clubs or teams sell candy or cookies to raise funds?

In Monty Python's The Life of Brian, a reluctant messiah stands on a rampart addressing the masses below: "Look, you've got it all wrong!" he cries. "You don't need to follow me. You don't need to follow anybody! You've got to think for yourselves. You're all individuals!" "Yes! We're all individuals!" the masses repeat in unison. Frustrated, he thinks, No, no. "You're all different!" he says. "Yes, we are all different!" they reply together. One bewildered man in the crowd turns to those around him and says, "I'm not . . ." and the others gang up to reprimand him: "Shhh!"

That's how orthodoxy works, and our schools will go deeper every time they encourage students to keep their eyes and minds open and to challenge dogma and convention of every kind.

14. Live in the present tense

Children and youth are living life itself; they are not experiencing half-a-life in preparation for some real life to be stepped into some day. And the best preparation for a meaningful future life is living a meaningful present life, right here and right now. Happiness leads to more happiness; confidence builds more confidence. In the schools we need, learning is not a bitter medicine hurriedly swallowed on someone else's promise that it will be good for you someday. In fact, "preparation" is a bent and broken frame for teaching and learning, and so the work of these schools will never be justified by reference to it.

Learning is its own justification—it must be infused with urgency and immediacy. While it is often raggedy, improvisational, and uneven, it must be relevant in its own right. We look to the past for insight and understanding, and we look to the future with longing and desire. But we are fully alive today—this is it. Don't postpone joy.

15. Unite hand and head

The separation of the manual from the mental is a false distinction, and profoundly alienating. We are whole beings with hearts and minds and spirits and bodies, and we should not accept a bright line between hand and head. The schools we deserve will purposefully engage hearts, heads, and hands as students forge their own pathways into a wider, shared world. W.E.B. DuBois once noted that a powerful education is not about making "men into carpenters," but insisting that "carpenters can become men," by which he meant that manual workers could enjoy opera, read poetry, write plays, make murals, or play the cello, just as intellectuals could learn to harvest avocados or make lentil soup and stir-fry or repair a bridge; all could become diverse and fully three-dimensional, entirely capable of naming their own predicaments, asking their own questions, contributing to the common good, and constructing their own lives.

I worked at shipyards in California and Florida for many years as a young man. And even though I was unloading cargo or cleaning the double-bottoms on huge cargo ships for 8–12 hours a day, I never stopped reading or seeing movies or going to museums or wondering about matters large and small and talking with my friends and fellow workers about things all day long. So whenever I hear politicians say empty-headed things like we need more carpenters and welders as opposed to more philosophers, I scratch my shipyard-working/philosophical head. Must one either be a welder or a philosopher? Shouldn't we aspire to be both?

The shipyard was filled with philosophers, and our extended, continuing conversations over lunch covered the waterfront from raising kids and negotiating relationships to sex and aging, from racism and male supremacy to religion, politics, and the meaning of life; they were intermittently funny, slyly subversive, openly rebellious, silly and sharp. But one thing is sure: If philosophy is a search for truth and meaning, we were doing philosophy while we toted those bales.

The poet and playwright Bertolt Brecht urged workers to "Study from bottom up," because they should be ready to "take the leadership." Start wherever you are, he said, and never think it's too late: "You must prepare to take command now!" And no matter what the difficulties or obstacles, learning must be part of every life, for study is indispensable to the future society—"Study, man in exile! Study, man in the prison! Study, wife in your kitchen! Study, old-age pensioner! . . . You who starve, reach for a book: it will be a weapon." Question everything, interrogate everything, challenge whatever offends your experience or your soul.

16. Organize opportunities to do and to make

Author, actor, builder, engineer, inventor, organizer, cook, mathematician, farmer, composer—these roles allow youth to wield essential tools against propaganda, political agendas, dogma, and all manner of impositions and stereotypes. Real work seeks authenticity: to do and to make are essential allies of critical, engaged, and vibrant minds. Doing and making enhances a sense of being fully alive, a work in progress born into a world in motion.

17. Prompt fearlessness

In the schools we need, students will be main actors in constructing their own educations, not simply the objects of a regime of discipline and punish; education will be decoupled from the inadequate and illegitimate "meritocracy model," and the public good will be understood more fundamentally. Instead of schooling as credentialing, sorting, gate-keeping, and controlling, our schools will enable *all* students to become smarter, more capable of negotiating our complex world, more able to work effectively in community and across communities to innovate and initiate with courage and creativity. We will re-examine core personal and ethical values in order to make more thoughtful, caring, and productive life choices. In the schools we deserve, no power is too big to challenge, no injustice too small to ignore. This will require audacity—from teachers, families, communities, and students—to build insurgent spaces focused on that we know we need rather than what we're told we must endure.

18. Resist the notion that education is a K–12 or K–16 affair

In the schools we need, everyone will be learning and everyone will be teaching, side by side, and hand in hand. There will be no hard division between teachers and students; rather there will be a gathering of student-teachers and teacher-students—everyone learning, everyone teaching all the time. As time passes, it's true, the young become the old as our stories steadily unfold—that's the way of life. And it's also true that there was once a time for each of us when everything seemed possible, and there will come a time when nothing at all is possible. But while we are here, suspended for a moment in the light, we do what we can: We teach and we learn, we sing the seasons and we dance the dialectic, we love and we live.

19. Pursue the production of human beings, not things

The schools we deserve will be oriented toward liberation and enlightenment as living forces and powerful aspirations, and will focus efforts, then, not on the production of things, but on the production of fully developed human beings who are capable of controlling and transforming their own lives; citizens and residents who see themselves as valued and valuable, a sovereign part of the whole, and can participate actively in public life; people who can open their eyes and awaken themselves and others as they think and act ethically in an ever-changing world. These schools will encourage students to make a difference, to develop the capacity to constantly interrogate the world and the courage to act upon whatever the known demands. Daily activity, then, will be transformed from rote boredom and endlessly alienating routines into something that is eye-popping and mind-blowing—always opening doors, opening minds, and opening hearts as students forge new pathways into a wider world.

There is a powerful letter making its way around Facebook and various online sites, purportedly first posted by an anonymous elementary school principal and addressed to students and families just as kids received their standardized test scores:

I'm concerned that these tests don't assess all of what it is that makes each of you unique. The people who created these tests and score them don't know each of you the way your teachers do, the way I hope I do, and certainly not the way your families do. They don't know that many of you speak two languages. They don't know that you can play a musical instrument or that you can dance or paint a picture. They don't know that your friends count on you to be there for them or that your laughter can brighten the dreariest day. They don't know that you write poetry or songs, play or participate in sports, wonder about the future, or that sometimes you take care of your little brother or sister after school. They don't know that you have traveled to a really neat place or that you know how to tell a great story or that you really love spending time with special family members and friends. They don't know that you can be trustworthy, kind or thoughtful, and that you try, every day, to do your very best. The scores you get will tell you something, but they will not tell you everything. There are many ways of being smart.

Human beings are three-dimensional, and good for this principal for underlining that fact, and encouraging students and their families to embrace the obvious and not be derailed by something reductive and petty.

20. See and do art

The arts are too often small and marginalized in schools, and this is a gathering catastrophe, not only for students and teachers, but for our common future as well. The arts invite us to look from a range of angles, to dive into contradictions, disagreements, silences, negation, denials, inconsistencies, confusion, challenges, turmoil, puzzlement, commotion, ambiguities, paradoxes, disputes, uncertainty, and every kind of muddle in order to see anew. The arts will be at the center and in every corner of the schools we deserve.

Life begins in wonder and so does art—education too. The arts allow children and youth to assemble tentative answers to the deepest questions, and over time to develop more sophisticated and dynamic ones. The arts offer an invitation to become the agent of your own story, the author of your own life, or the actor in your own film as opposed to some anonymous walk-on in someone else's worn out and clichéd scripts. Art—including the art of constructing our own lives—is essential to our shared human experience.

21. Embrace mystery

We are, in spite of the existential feel of things and our own natural narcissism, finite beings plunging through an infinite space and gazing toward an expanding heaven. We are in the middle of things, and at the end of nothing—the unseen, the hidden, the mysterious, the invisible, the indefinite, the unfamiliar, the unknown, the unheard of, and the forgotten are vast, while our various maps of the known world are limited, paltry, and, mostly castles in the sky. Learning to question, to interrogate, to experiment, to wonder and to wander, to construct and create—this is the sturdiest foundation upon which to build an education of purpose for a free people.

In the schools we deserve, big questions can be followed to their outer limits because the pressure to "cover the curriculum" is pushed to the background—"curriculum" is transformed into a problem-posing and question-asking activity, and the pretense of "coverage" is thoroughly rejected. The schools we need will be simple, dark, and deep.

◇   ◇   ◇

Twenty-one gestures toward a vision of the kind of schools all children and youth deserve. Twenty-one baby steps forward.

And this is only a first draft—no, merely the draft of a draft of a draft. Dive in and lend a hand; help make this a more complete and comprehensive frame, a more useful outline for you and your people, and a more sturdy scaffolding for the necessary work ahead.

It's within our power to build learning communities that no one will have to suffer through, schools that kids won't need to recover from. There are hopeful bits and pieces everywhere, and we can stimulate and stir up these features wherever we are and whenever we find them, blowing on the embers, nourishing and encouraging whatever tentative flickers and flashes we uncover. After all, a single spark can ignite a prairie fire.

FIVE

◇◇◇◇◇◇◇◇◇◇◇◇◇◇◇◇◇◇◇◇◇◇◇◇◇◇◇◇

Be realistic: Demand the impossible.

The question of what's possible arises whenever people organize or mobilize themselves to push for change. What's realistic? What can we hope for, and what can be won? How? There's the danger of overreach, to be sure, of seeking changes that are unrealizable because the material conditions of life on the ground cannot possibly support or sustain them. But the more frequent (and perhaps greater) danger is *under*reach, the failure to articulate a deep enough vision, to understand the root causes of the problems we want to address and overcome, or to fully trust and be willing to amplify the potential energy of people who deserve something better and long to change themselves and revolutionize their world. In those cases we don't stretch far enough or push hard enough; we become overly concerned with appearing reasonable or we self-censor and trim our own sails, worried that we will undermine our credibility by demanding a bit too much of utopia; we settle for anemic reforms when we could have won more long-lasting and more meaningful transformations.

Imagining schools that I (or "we," if you'll seize the time and join the drive) would joyously and courageously sign up to fight for and fashion right here, right now, opens up a vision of spaces—or spaces within spaces—that are small and personal; that honor and support the work of students and teachers; that use families, museums, and studios as models more than commerce or industry or the military (scale, interaction, exploration); that are interdisciplinary and integrated, agile and grounded; and that offer real opportunities for students to choose what to pursue, investigate, create, or construct. A workshop or a gallery, a playground vibrating with sports and games or an atelier overflowing with opportunities to make art, a laboratory for experimentation or a theater for myriad untold performances—imagine the palaces of learning and life we could build if we mobilized and organized and focused ourselves on that essential work.

A delightful cartoon from a few years ago bore the caption "If they'd had Prozac in the 19th century"; it depicts the possibility of several revolutionary thinkers blitzing out on drugs and toning down their ideas: Edgar Allen Poe gazing at a raven and saying, "Nice birdie;" Marx in his library writing, "I think capitalism can work out its kinks." It's silly, of course, but it makes me want to stay far away from Prozac, metaphorically and for real.

Most American settlers thought that King George and the colonies could work out their kinks, but the revolutionaries of 1776 went deeper and made the truly radical demand—Independence! Liberal reformers later fought to end the North Atlantic slave trade and the expansion of slavery into the west—worthwhile reforms to be sure—but the Abolitionists refused to be side-tracked by partial solutions or entirely satisfied with small improvements that left an evil system intact—Freedom!

Let's take heart and dream big: If we storm the heavens and come up short, at least we will have tried; if we aim low and soften our enthusiasm, we could find ourselves betraying, not only the better angels of ourselves, but the hopes of future generations as well. Better to have danced out on a limb and fallen to the ground than to have never reached at all.

We need to practice a two-step approach: one foot planted firmly in the mud and the muck of the world as it is, and one foot striding freely toward the world as it could be or should be—a world worth fighting for. That means that we engage fully here and now: In our classrooms we work each day to become better teachers, more geared into the growth and development of the children before us; in our unions we fight for recognition and respect and excellent working conditions, knowing that good working conditions *are* good teaching conditions and that good teaching conditions *are* good learning conditions; in our communities we make common cause with parents and students, natural allies and comrades-in-arms, who are mobilizing to keep public education alive and thriving and to keep public schools open and accessible. All of this day by day, and all the while keeping our eyes on the prize: Free Schools for Free People!

An old friend who's a big-time criminal defense attorney explained to me once how he set his fees: "I look the client over, consider my own circumstances, close my eyes, and pick a number out of thin air—if the bum's knees don't buckle, I guessed low." That's another useful guideline for us: Our demands should reflect our best thinking, our considered judgment, but in the end we must be able to observe the bum's knees crumpling—call it "the knee-buckling standard!"

Let's return for a moment to John Dewey's Utopians; they'd speculated that the educational system Dewey described to them must have meant that the schools from his time and place were embedded in an socioeconomic system based on personal acquisition, and that that system had become so powerful that it pulled all that was within reach into its swirling vortex, remaking everything in its own image. This is another key insight for us, and something we need to keep in mind as we imagine or plan our insurgencies in the schools: Schools always reflect and reveal larger social/cultural/economic/historical realities.

This means that if you know something about any particular society, you can predict with some confidence the shape and structure of its schools, and, conversely, if you look closely enough at the schools, you will see a shadowy likeness of the larger society: An ancient agrarian village apprenticed its young for full participation in the rustic world of agriculture and animal husbandry; schools in a theocracy preached faithfulness and piety and devotion; apartheid South Africa built beautiful dominions of learning and small state-of-the-art classes for White kids and overcrowded, dilapidated, and ill-equipped classes for the African kids. And remember Dickens's Victorian schools with their "imperial gallons of facts."

It also tells us that any dramatic change in society will necessarily echo in the educational arena, just as struggles to change the schools will ripple out into the larger society. Again, schools serve societies and societies set up schools—one side of that twosome can't shake or shift impressively while leaving the other standing entirely still. It makes sense, then, that schools based on free inquiry or unrestricted engagement with literature have been consistently closed down in countries dominated by orthodox religious authorities, or that for decades alternative schools built on cooperation and respect, for example, have always had a terrible time surviving within a larger social context of cutthroat competition. The ethical heart of one is in mortal combat with the driving force of the other.

James Baldwin said it clearly in his now-famous "A Talk to Teachers" in 1963:

> Now the crucial paradox which confronts us here is that the whole process of education occurs within a social framework and is designed to perpetuate the aims of society. Thus, for example, the boys and girls who were born during the era of the Third Reich, when educated to the purposes of the Third Reich, became barbarians. The paradox of education is precisely this—that as one begins to become conscious one begins to examine the society in which he [or she] is being educated. The purpose of education, finally, is to create in a person the ability to look at the world for himself, to make his own decisions, to say to himself this is black or this is white, to decide for himself whether there is a God in heaven or not. To ask questions of the universe, and then learn to live with those questions, is the way he achieves his own identity. But no society is really anxious to have that kind of person around. What societies really, ideally, want is a citizenry which will simply obey the rules of society. If a society succeeds in this, that society is about to perish. The obligation of anyone who thinks of himself as responsible is to examine society and try to change it and to fight it—at no matter what risk. This is the only hope society has. This is the only way societies change.

Those who think the schools can be fundamentally transformed while the larger society chugs along untouched are indulging in fantasy; but those who think society must be radically transformed before the serious work of creating more humane schools can begin are misreading history and imposing a linear and mechanistic logic on a landscape that is much more complex and dynamic than they may think. The truth is that schools are a natural site of social struggle—they are where we ask ourselves profound questions about what's worthwhile to know and experience, and what constitutes the good life; they are where we imagine and work to construct a future; and they are where young people gather to discover their own ways forward as they (metaphorically perhaps—but who knows?) put the society they inherited on trial.

Young people here and across the globe have risen up to change the world—indicting the status quo as a kind of state of emergency—from Little Rock to Birmingham, Soweto to Tiananmen, Palestine to Chiapas, Wounded Knee to Cairo. The ignition switch for rebellion has time after time been found within the schools. With their radical impulse to revolt, a spirit of hopefulness and possibility, their laser-like insights into the hypocrisies of the adult world, youth have propelled themselves forward, breaking the rules and dancing to a different tune, providing insight and inspiration as catalysts, activists, and organizers for change. They've been ignored and ridiculed, written off and repressed, co-opted and attacked, and still they rise, exercising their stubborn agency again and again, offering themselves as a fresh and searing force for equality, racial justice, environmental sanity, economic fairness, recognition, and dignity.

As young people in New Orleans, South Central LA, Detroit, Philadelphia, the West Side of Chicago, or many points in-between discover and develop their own blossoming sense of agency, they begin to see themselves as full and central actors in the world. No longer adjuncts in society or objects for constant manipulation—directed to where they may or may not go, instructed about when they may speak and which books they may read, restricted in what matters they may or may not cross-examine, told what to study, what time they may or may not eat, and when to pee or shit—they begin to question the nature of the schooling they're offered, and the schools of poverty (for many, materially, for others, spiritually and intellectually) they're required to attend.

They realize, perhaps intuitively at first, that as free and full human beings they are inherently (and not contingently) valuable.

They feel themselves to be in motion, swirling through a vibrant living history, and they find that both they and the world they inherit are works in progress—still under construction. If they come to believe that they don't need anyone's permission to interrogate the world, watch out! Interrogating the real conditions of their lives will allow young folks to step out of subjugation and into history. The wardens of the status quo will understand that act of questioning to be a challenge, and they are not wrong. To the oppressed and exploited, the everyday functioning of the system is itself an act of violence—it must be resisted. To the wardens, the resistance must be quelled. The conflict is on.

Our schools show us who we are—the good, the bad, and the ugly—beyond rhetoric or self-congratulatory platitudes. If some of what we see in our schools is not as we would like it, well, we can search for all kinds of explanations and justifications. We can, in our defense, retreat to our good intentions; or we might, more positively, conclude that some things *need* to be changed—in schools and in society. We might decide to join hands with others, then, and work together to create those changes. Getting there is the real challenge.

Enter the fraught but fascinating territory of agitation and organizing and movement building, for even a cursory glance at history shows us that broad and deep transformations are always the result of mobilized popular movements, the real engines of social change. Lyndon Johnson passed the most far-reaching civil rights legislation since Reconstruction, but he was never part of the Black Freedom Movement. Franklin Delano Roosevelt led huge legislative advances in workers' rights and social welfare, but he was not part of the labor movement. And Abraham Lincoln, who issued the Emancipation Proclamation ending chattel slavery in the Confederacy, never belonged to an abolitionist party. These three presidents are remembered for earth-shaking accomplishments, and yet none of them acted alone, and in fact each was reacting to intense and sustained fire from below. Most of us have no way into the places of official power—the White House, the Congress, or the Pentagon—but we have easy access to other locations of real power: the school and the classroom, for example, the community and the neighborhood, the workplace and the street. We make a terrible mistake when we look longingly at the sites of power we have no admittance to while ignoring the places and people right in front of us who can be mobilized to create deep and lasting change.

We cannot bring a social movement into being through willpower alone, of course, but neither does it make sense to wait patiently for a movement to present itself as if it had sprung fully-formed from the head of Zeus. The world we need and desire will be forged in action by people struggling for something better, working together in common cause, developing and transforming themselves as they gather momentum and energy in the hopeful tradition of revolution. We must open our eyes, we must act, and we must rethink and start again. The painstaking work begins now and can never really be finished.

Part of movement building involves breaking from the TINA trap: There-Is-No-Alternative. The privileged and the powerful insist that we accept on faith that this is the best of all possible worlds, and that even with all of its imperfections, it is inevitable and, well, There-Is-No-Alternative. Our job is to posit compelling alternatives, to demonstrate that the world as such is a choice, and then to break from the phony nonchoices that characterize so much political talk in our country. We need to reframe the issues. In education, for example, when the multiple-choice test asks whether I'm in favor of preserving the status quo or destroying public education, my checkmark goes to "none of the above." I need to break the frame. My write-in answer offers an alternative: Free Schools for Free People.

Because teaching has been the center of my life, I tend to see education as linked to every other important social issue. Reforming criminal justice touches on education issues; racial justice has an educational aspect; environmental awareness, human rights, gender equity—education is a part of everything.

When I mentioned this to my partner, a law professor and children's advocate, a peace and human rights activist, she said that while I may be right, it was also true that every contemporary issue of importance was connected to human rights: immigration, Black Lives Matter!, sexual assault, the status of children, war, man-made climate change, education, and more. Our activist friends from the environmental justice movement say the same thing, and so do the participants from Occupy. Go deep enough and it's true: Everything is connected to everything else at the root.

The lesson for movement builders is this: We need to reject the logic of power; we need to rethink and recast issues in more robust and humane frames; we need to connect the issues in order to find our natural allies and comrades and in order to develop a more comprehensive view. Whoever we are and wherever we work and play, we must remind ourselves that movements don't make themselves. It's up to each and all of us to pop up every day with our minds set on freedom, and to commit to movement building as a regular and required part of what we do.

◇   ◇   ◇

Beyond the clamor of the noisy school reformers—the marketeers and the banksters with their hedge-fund homies—beneath the clutter of educational policy, and below the radar of the paid chattering pundits and the boisterous, bottom-feeding politicians, lies something elegant and precious: teachers and students in relationship; an endless journey in an ongoing world; an ethical and intellectual transaction underway. It's the universe of teaching and learning, the domain of schools and classrooms, parks and playgrounds, gymnasiums and community centers, street corners and houses of worship, and it's brought to life, quietly and simply, in millions and millions of daily encounters in every corner of the globe. This is the country of the young—dazzling, trembling, and real.

At its best teaching is about enlightenment and liberation, opening possibilities of freedom and pathways to truth, and it is first of all a relationship, excruciatingly complex and wildly diverse in action and application. It's a relationship practiced in a specific site, a tangible here and now, always brought to life in the dynamic, surging, transient, imperfect, and fugitive spaces we share—this community or another, this prairie or that field, this classroom or that other one, this street or that pathway. But whatever intersections we occupy, wherever we find ourselves tossed up on the shores of history, if we are to be conscientious and effective we must open our eyes to those who are all around us, conscious of the commitments we bring and the values we want to share and develop through those relationships.

I like this list of commitments—called "Ten Commandments"—that the British philosopher Bertrand Russell compiled for himself and published in the *New York Times* in 1951:

- Do not feel absolutely certain of anything.
- Do not think it worthwhile to proceed by concealing evidence, for the evidence is sure to come to light.
- Never try to discourage thinking for you are sure to succeed.
- When you meet with opposition . . . endeavor to overcome it by argument and not by authority, for a victory dependent upon authority is unreal and illusory.
- Have no respect for the authority of others, for there are always contrary authorities to be found.
- Do not use power to suppress opinions you think pernicious, for if you do the opinions will suppress you.
- Do not fear to be eccentric in opinion, for every opinion now accepted was once eccentric.
- Find more pleasure in intelligent dissent than in passive agreement, for, if you value intelligence as you should, the former implies a deeper agreement than the latter.
- Be scrupulously truthful, even if the truth is inconvenient, for it is more inconvenient when you try to conceal it.
- Do not feel envious of the happiness of those who live in a fool's paradise, for only a fool will think that it is happiness.

Every teacher can make a short list of commandments or commitments for herself or himself now—a reminder that can be taped to the refrigerator or the bathroom mirror—to be consulted quickly every morning before heading out.

My list—subject to endless revision—begins like this:

- ◆ I will make every effort to see each student as my teacher, a work in progress, and a unique human being—the one of one—to be celebrated and treated always with awe and respect.
- ◆ I will never treat a student as an object or a thing.
- ◆ I will strive to create a society of respect and compassion in our classroom.
- ◆ I will do my best to connect the community of the classroom with widening circles of community beyond the classroom.
- ◆ I will make "learning to live together" a top priority.
- ◆ I will work to create an environment that's deep enough and wide enough so that everyone finds something familiar and something strange, something to nourish them and something to challenge them.
- ◆ I will attempt to always connect the known to deeper and wider ways of knowing.
- ◆ I will provide a dynamic range of ways for students to interrogate the universe.
- ◆ I will try to live out and model the values I espouse, including honesty, courage, integrity, curiosity, initiative, tolerance, kindness, fairness, and justice.
- ◆ I know I will fall short—and so I will end each day with a critical review of what I need to improve upon by tomorrow at the latest, and I'll begin each day forgiving myself for yesterday's shortcomings, missed opportunities, and failures.

My commitments sum up in brief the direction and rhythm, the pathway already outlined: Become a student of my students first, and create a community through dialogue; love my neighbors;

question everything; defend the downtrodden; challenge and nourish myself and others; seek balance.

I want every teacher to develop his or her own wild and eclec-
tic and dynamic list, something to hold onto through stormy seas,
something to reach for when lost or lonely, and something to inspire you as you try to teach with conscience in a troubled and
imperfect world.

Here's Walt Whitman in one of his many propulsive prefaces to
Leaves of Grass:

This is what you shall do:

Love the earth and sun and the animals, despise riches, give alms to
everyone that asks, stand up for the stupid and crazy, devote your
income and labor to others, hate tyrants, argue not concerning God,
have patience and indulgence toward the people, take off your hat
to nothing known or unknown or to any man or number of men, go
freely with powerful uneducated persons and with the young and with
the mothers of families, re-examine all you have been told at school
or church or in any book, dismiss whatever insults your own soul, and
your very flesh shall be a great poem and have the richest fluency not
only in its words but in the silent lines of its lips and face and between
the lashes of your eyes and in every motion and joint of your body . . .

Nice start, Walt. That's a list to laminate and carry along in your
backpack, or another list to tape to your wall. It's written to poets,
but it stands as worthwhile advice to free teachers, too. Your list
must be yours, created by you and for you, tailored to your mind's
eye and your heart's desire, a list that only you in your uniqueness
can possibly make.

◇   ◇   ◇

To be enslaved is to be measured and estimated, inspected and evaluated, regulated and corrected, brainwashed and propagandized,
threatened and prodded and punished. It's to have your agency

ignored or constrained or systematically crushed. To trudge toward freedom is to overthrow all of that through self-activity, an insurgency that involves seizing and practicing your own agency, stepping into history not as an object—a fraction of a human being, or three-fifths of a person—not as a label or a collection of deficits or someone else's imposed statistical profile, but as a fully realized and three-dimensional human being.

Thousands, tens of thousands, and millions right now share a faith that injustice can be opposed and justice aspired to, that human solidarity and connectedness can become a living force, that a spirit of outrage can be tempered with vast feelings of love and generosity, and that a full and passionate embrace of the life we're given can be combined with an eagerness to move forward striving to build a worldwide beloved community.

The country is as it is—a mass of contradictions and tragedies; rich with beauty and human accomplishment, vicious with human denial; an organism that drains us and replenishes us at the same time, gives us life and kills us—and it's asking us to dive in: study, imagine, ask difficult questions, read, learn, organize, talk to strangers, mobilize, and display your ethical aspirations publicly.

Turn out all the lights and ignite one small candle in any corner. That tiny little light held aloft anywhere challenges the darkness everywhere. One candle. We can always do something, and something is where we begin.

The tools are everywhere—humor and art; protest and spectacle; the quiet, patient intervention and the angry and urgent thrust—and the rhythm of and recipe for activism is always the same: We open our eyes and look unblinkingly at the immense and dynamic world we find before us; we are astonished by the beauty and horrified at the suffering all around us; we organize ourselves, link hands with others, dive in, speak up, and act out; we doubt that our efforts made any important difference whatsoever, and so we rethink, recalibrate, look again, and dive in once more.

In the current contested space of public "school reform" it can seem that the privatizers and the marketeers have all the power: the hedge-fund dollars, the foundation endorsements, an amen-chorus of the for-profit media and the chattering class, and the mindless acquiescence of major players in the two dominant political parties. This is a lot, and it can feel overwhelming, but look more closely at what they're missing after decades of wielding the sweet, sweet carrot and the big stick: They have not won over a majority of teachers and students or parents and community members; they have not quelled the opposition or the resistance; they have not developed a compelling or coherent moral argument for destroying the public education system and replacing it with a string of privately managed profit centers. It's as clear as ever that schools and classrooms are contested spaces and that, in spite of everything, the wind is blowing hard against the corporate takeover.

Curriculum, teaching, and education are arenas of struggle as well as hope: struggle because they stir in us the need to look at the world anew, to question what we have created, to wonder what is worthwhile for human beings to know and experience; and hope because they gesture toward the future, toward the impending, toward the coming of the new. This is where we ask how we might engage, enlarge, and change our lives, and it is, then, where we confront our dreams and struggle over notions of the good life, where we try to comprehend, apprehend, or possibly even change the world. Public education is a natural site of contestation—sometimes restrained, other times in full eruption—over questions of justice.

Like every muscular, compelling, and layered concept, *social justice* is difficult to sum up and quite impossible to define definitively. More process than calculation, more journey than destination, social justice is a stated goal shared by folks from the Left and the Right, from the Pope to the Dalai Lama, from social revolutionaries to community organizers, and it's an impulse that resists easy answers and defies breezy responses. There is simply no getting to the bottom of it, once and for all—social justice is too dynamic, too contentious, too dense, too on-the-move and in-the-mix.

Social justice can be thrilling and just as often surprising and disorienting—it stretches toward the infinite, embracing the far-flung strivings of wildly diverse peoples in different times and places, under vastly different circumstances, using different tools and tactics and methods and approaches to achieve greater freedom, fairness, equity, access, agency, openness, sustainability, and recognition. That human striving, that hunger for justice, is awakened when people recognize, often fleetingly or glancingly at first, that the forces pressing down upon us—forces of oppression and exploitation, racism and discrimination, displacement and erasure—are neither natural nor immutable. We open our eyes and notice that things could be otherwise; we resist; we rise up angry.

The social justice activists who inspire and move me again and again are the ones who defend the weak, defy oppressive or even imperfect authority, criticize orthodoxy and dogma, stereotype and received wisdom of every kind. They are often freedom fighters who lean hard against the idea that life or learning must be an arid, dry, self-referencing and self-satisfied affair, a mechanical trivial pursuit of the obvious; they resist deference, didacticism, ego and complacency in a heartless world, prisons and border guards and walls—whether in our own minds or in the lives of our students, whether in Texas or in Palestine—and quarantines, deletions, and closures. They welcome the unknown, the marvelous, the poetics of resistance, history, and agency. They provide frames for mapping a world that could be but is not yet, a place of joy and justice, powered by love.

Awareness and wide-awakeness—this is the starting point of struggles for justice, but it is not the end. We open our eyes and allow ourselves a sense of wonder and astonishment: There is loveliness all around us, aching beauty, yes, and even flashes of ecstasy; there is horror in every direction as well, appalling injustices and pain, the unnecessary suffering that human beings visit upon one another. We feel the need to speak up and act out, and this is the rhythm of rebellion: pay attention; be astonished; act. Add the need to doubt that whatever you saw or did or said was adequate or complete, and then the charge to rethink and start over, and you've got the rhythm of revolution: pay attention, be astonished, act up, and doubt. Repeat for a lifetime.

The great rebel Rosa Luxemburg, jailed for her opposition to World War I, lived her life to that rhythm. She sent a letter from prison to a friend and comrade who'd complained to her that their revolutionary work was suffering terribly without Luxemburg's day-to-day leadership. First, she wrote, stop whining—excellent advice in any circumstance. She went on to urge her friend to be more of a *mensch*. Oh, I can't define *mensch* for you, she said, but what I mean is that you should strive to be a person who loves your own life enough to appreciate the sunset and the sunrise, to enjoy a bottle of wine over dinner with friends, or to take a walk by the sea. But you must also love the world enough, she continued, to put your shoulder on history's great wheel when history demands it. Working that out is a daily challenge, but it's the way forward toward commitment and balance.

Love your own life. Love the world. Be a *mensch!*

◇◇◇◇◇◇◇◇◇◇◇◇◇◇◇◇◇◇◇◇◇◇◇◇◇◇◇◇

A Few Essential Additions

Books are call'd for, and supplied, on the assumption that the process of reading is not a half sleep, but, in the highest sense an exercise, a gymnast's struggle; that the reader is to do something for himself, must be on the alert, must himself or herself construct indeed the poem, argument, history, metaphysical essay—the text furnishing the hints, the clue, the start or framework. Not the book needs so much to be the complete thing, but the reader of the book does. That were to make a nation of supple and athletic minds, well-train'd, intuitive, used to depend on themselves, and not on a few coteries of writers.

—Walt Whitman

You think your pain and your heartbreak are unprecedented in the history of the world, but then you read. It was books that taught me that the things that tormented me most were the very things that connected me with all the people who were alive, or who had ever been alive.

—James Baldwin

FOR FURTHER READING

Ta-Nehisi Coats: *Between the World and Me.* (2015). New York, NY: Spiegel & Grau.

Paulo Freire: *Pedagogy of the Oppressed* (30th anniversary edition). (2000). New York, NY: Bloomsbury.

Kevin Kumashiro: *Bad Teacher* (2012). New York, NY: Teachers College Press.

Junot Diaz: *The Brief and Wondrous Life of Oscar Wao.* (2007). New York, NY: Riverhead Books.

Jay Gillin: *Educating for Insurgency: The Roles of Young People in Schools of Poverty.* (2014). Oakland, CA: AK Press.

William Ayers and Ryan Alexander-Tanner: *To Teach: The Journey, in Comics.* (2010). New York, NY: Teachers College Press.

Mike Rose: *Why School?: Reclaiming Education for All of Us.* (2014). New York, NY: The New Press.

Joel Westheimer: *What Kind of Citizen?* (2015). New York, NY: Teachers College Press.

Julie Diamond: *Kindergarten: A Teacher, Her Students, and a Year of Learning.* (2008). New York, NY: The New Press.

Gloria Ladson-Billings: *The Dreamkeepers: Successful Teachers of African American Children.* (2009). San Francisco, CA: John Wiley & Sons.

Angela Valenzuela: *Subtractive Schooling: U.S.–Mexican Youth and the Politics of Caring.* (1999). Albany, NY: State University of New York Press.

REFERENCES

Baldwin, J. (1985). A talk to teachers. In *The price of the ticket: Collected nonfiction, 1948–1985.* New York, NY: St. Martin's Press.

Ginzburg, N. (1985). *The little virtues.* New York: Arcade.

Klein, R. (2015, July 30). "After facing backlash, AP U.S. History course revised to emphasize American ideals." *Huffington Post.* Retrieved from huffingtonpost.com/entry/ap-us-history-framework_55ba1f15e4b0af35367a538d

Lessing, D. (1995). *Under my skin: Volume one of my autobiography, to 1949.* New York, NY: Harper Perennial.

Lessing, D. (2008). *The golden notebook.* New York, NY: Harper Perennial.

Neill, A. S. (1992). *Summerhill School: A new view of childhood* (A. Lamb, Ed.). New York, NY: St. Martin's Griffin.

Porter, E. (2015, March 24). "Grading teachers by the test." *New York Times.* Retrieved from nyti.ms/1BhHQtJ

Schubert, W. H. (2010). *Love, justice, and education: John Dewey and the Utopians.* Charlotte, NC: Information Age.

Soep, L., & Chávez, V. (2010). *Drop that knowledge: Youth radio stories.* Los Angeles, CA: University of California Press.

About the Author

William Ayers is Distinguished Professor of Education and Senior University Scholar at the University of Illinois at Chicago (retired), education activist, and bestselling author of *Teaching the Taboo: Courage and Imagination in the Classroom* (with Rick Ayers), *To Teach: The Journey of a Teacher, Third Edition*, and *To Teach: The Journey, in Comics* (with Ryan Alexander-Tanner).